# THE TRUE CRIME OF MODERN DATING:

## A Woman, a Pattern, and a Trail of Dating Casualties

By

A.K. Warren

This work is nonfiction. Names, identifying details, and certain circumstances have been changed to protect the privacy of individuals. Any resemblance to actual persons, living or dead, is coincidental.

This book is intended for informational and reflective purposes only and does not constitute professional, psychological, or legal advice.

ISBN: 979-8-9943422-0-6 (Paperback)
First edition, 2026

Published independently by Warren Studio, LLC
Digitally published in the United States of America

Cover design and interior layout by Impulse Strategies Inc.

For my daughter.

You are the reason I believe in love. Your heart, your courage, your light… they give me hope for a world where love looks more like respect, laughter, and safety. May your journey be different from mine but just as full of truth.

**CONTENT NOTE:**

This book explores themes related to modern dating, divorce, emotional manipulation, infidelity, and personal identity. Some chapters include discussions of sexual coercion, emotional and physical harm, and experiences that may be distressing for some readers.

These moments are written with care and intention, but reader discretion is advised. Please take whatever space you need while reading and prioritize your own well-being.

# THE CASE LOG

# OPENING STATEMENT

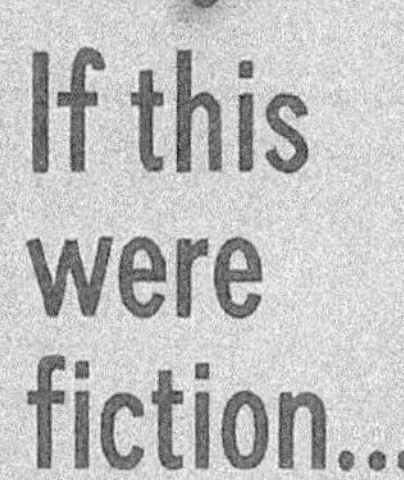

# OPENING STATEMENT:
## Confessions of a Repeat Offender

---

If this were fiction, I'd tone it down.
If this were fiction, I'd make myself prettier.

I'd leave out the part where my great-great-great-great uncle was Bat Masterson, a gunslinging lawman-turned-legend from my mother's side of the family. I'd downplay the part where my grandmother walked away from East Coast money and a broken marriage in the 1950s to raise two kids alone in the Deep South and marry a survivalist from Alaska. Those stories? Too wild for fiction.

But here we are. And none of it's made up.

These are my roots. A legacy of tough, talented matriarchs who served their family and community, all while navigating the professional world with charm and grit. Sometimes partnered, sometimes solo. Independence wasn't aspirational in my family. It was expected.

And me? I'm the youngest of two. A curious, curvy, creative soul raised between continents, cultures, and contradictions. Church basements and international airports. Faith and discipline. Curiosity and compliance. I learned early how to adapt, perform, and lead—skills that served me beautifully in school and business but didn't translate well in romantic relationships.

My father was an Air Force fighter pilot turned engineer. Charismatic. Strategic. The kind of man who filled a room and adored his wife out loud. He made sure I always knew I was loved and warned me early that "men are pigs." My mother was a force of nature—wife, volunteer, educator, counselor, hostess, pianist, dancer and believer. She walked her talk and modeled high standards, the living embodiment of everything a woman was supposed to be. My older brother was a rebel. Brilliant. Restless. Always pushing against systems that didn't fit. Always reminding me to learn from his mistakes.

As the baby of the family, I was protected and observant. I learned early which rules mattered and how to follow them well. I was all book smarts and no street smarts. Trusting. Optimistic. Determined. Always looking forward to the next adventure or challenge.

I assumed everyone was striving toward the same things as I was: faith, service, duty, success. Why wouldn't I? Everyone I ever knew said what they meant and kept their promises.

What I didn't understand—not yet—was how differently people played this game. Not everyone believed the things I did or measured worth the same way.

I believed goodness would be rewarded. That love would last just like my parents' did. That being married was proof you had done something right. At an early age, I also learned that beauty was part of that equation. Not in theory, but in practice. It mattered to my mother. It mattered to men. It mattered more than anyone ever liked to admit.

Beauty wasn't just admired. It was rewarded. I watched how differently the world responded when women were smaller. Prettier. Easier. I noticed how attention followed appearance, how forgiveness came faster, how doors opened a little more readily.

My problem was simple. I wasn't the pretty one.

So, when I met my future husband in college, I didn't see luck. I saw confirmation. I believed God was honoring my obedience, rewarding faith with permanence.

We were friends first, then got married a couple years after college. Five years later, we were in our first house and pregnant with our daughter. All confirmation of us following God's plan for our lives. Twelve years in, it was over. I was left with stretch marks and stories, determined to start again and get my life back on track.

I spent the next twelve years in the wild west of modern dating—dodging red flags, mistaking praise for partnership, falling in love too quickly, or not at all.

Then somewhere between heartbreak and hot girl summers, I realized the most consistent thing in all my dating disasters ... was me.

So, this book? It's not advice.
It's confession.
It's comedy.
It's a crime scene.

A forensic look at the loves that left me lonely, the ones that transformed my thinking, and the big "aha" moments that finally helped me stop being the victim of my own patterns.

You're about to read the dating case file of a woman raised to lead, taught to achieve, and conditioned to serve, who finally had to learn how to accept her own flaws and still be worthy of love.

And if that sounds like fiction, I get it.
But it's 100% true.

# SCENE OF THE CRIME

DIVORCE FILE

*You are the most amazing person I've ever known...*

# SCENE OF THE CRIME:

## When the Pattern Becomes the Partner

---

Every investigator needs a starting point. A moment when something just doesn't add up. This was mine.

I had been divorced for twelve years now. The exact length of my marriage. I don't know what I expected to happen when I crossed that threshold, but part of me thought some cosmic clock would reset. Like I'd finally "balance the books" on love and heartache somehow.

Spoiler alert: it didn't.

That same year, I was knee-deep in a self-imposed decluttering frenzy. Digitizing old files, tossing out half-used journals, and trying to let go of things that no longer served me. That's when I found it: a thick manila folder stuffed with the paper trail from the darkest years of my marriage. Letters to therapists. Emails to each other. Chat transcripts. Cry-for-help Word docs written at 2 a.m. when I couldn't sleep and couldn't scream.

At first, I tossed it into the "shred" pile. But curiosity is a nosy little gremlin. A couple days later, I was sitting cross-legged on the floor, flipping through the pages like a detective reviewing a cold case. I told myself I was looking for closure. Maybe I was looking for evidence.

Somewhere around page 48, I found it. The one line that stopped me mid-breath and rewrote my last decade of dating in an instant.

***"You are the most amazing person I've ever known, and you have always deserved better."***

It was written by my ex-husband. A man who had cheated, gaslit, and emotionally ghosted his way through a marriage where a child was present.

And here's the kicker: I believed him. Maybe I hadn't believed it then, but that was not in question now. I am amazing. I do deserve better. What shattered me wasn't the compliment. It was the contradiction.

***How could someone see me clearly and still choose to hurt me? How could someone believe I deserved better... and refuse to be better?***

And just like that, the emotional crime scene lit up like one of those black light investigations on CSI.

In the twelve years since that letter, I had been dating that ***exact*** contradiction: Men who adored me but abandoned me. Men who praised my strength then resented it. Men who said I was "too good for them" and proved it by treating me like I was disposable. And I kept mistaking their awe for intimacy. Their admiration for effort. Their high opinion of me as a substitute for showing up, choosing me, growing with me. The truth is, I wasn't just a victim of bad men. I was a repeat offender of my own pattern. I kept choosing familiar pain wrapped in flattering words. Trying to rewrite the ending to a story that had already told me how it goes.

And then there was the line I heard repeatedly:

***"You're just so... Intimidating."***

At first, I took it personally. I received it as sincere criticism revealing something about me that needed to be changed. Maybe I was too much. Too accomplished. Too opinionated. Too emotionally fluent. Too aware of what I wanted and unwilling to pretend otherwise. But let's be honest: that line is rarely about me. It's a mirror men hold up and can't bear to look into.

For a while, I tried to soften. I shrank. Smiled smaller. Gave disclaimers before I said something smart. I made room where I shouldn't have and still got left behind. Eventually, I stopped treating "intimidating" as an insult. I started treating it like a filter. The ones who can't handle it? Self-selected out.

I learned that "intimidating" was code for: You don't need me to feel complete. You won't laugh at my mediocre jokes out of politeness. You ask questions I don't want to answer. You hold me accountable. You take up space and expect me to take up mine, too.

And when a man says that and backs away, what he's doing is confessing: "You scare me because you already know you deserve more than I know how to give."

But here's the thing. It wasn't just them.

It wasn't only their insecurity or avoidance or lack of capacity. I have plenty of insecurities and limitations too. The pattern didn't start with them. It started with me.

It started in my formative years. It took root during my marriage. It was so deeply ingrained that I couldn't see how it was hindering my efforts to find a lasting relationship. Because patterns don't announce themselves with a single event. They reveal themselves through repetition—through outcomes that refuse to change, even when the players do.

The file I was holding in my hands wasn't just proof of my marital wreckage. It was the blueprint for everything that came after.

With my newfound clarity, it was time to pull the other case files out for a full review.

# THE INVESTIGATION BEGINS

# PART ONE:

## The Investigation Begins

---

Now the office is clear. The room is quiet.

Not the kind of quiet that feels empty, but the kind that comes after noise and chaos. After the dust finally settles.

I sit at my investigator's desk with a stack of dating files in front of me. Real ones. Thick. Dog-eared. Marked by time. Each crime scene labeled with a name, a season, and a version of me I barely recognize anymore. Some added weight. Others exposed where something was lost, stolen, or broken. A few handed me the truth like a knife I wasn't ready to hold.

But this isn't where the stories began.
It's where they're being reviewed.

Back then, I didn't know I was collecting evidence. I thought I was just living. Loving. Trying again. I didn't have language for patterns or frameworks for self-protection. All I had was hope, instinct, and the belief that honesty and effort would eventually lead to a happy ending.

Now, I see things differently.

Time does that. Distance sharpens things.
Healing clears the lens.

From here, I can see the through-lines I missed while I was inside the story.

The woman who lived these stories is not the woman reading them now. But to understand the evidence, I must remember the conditions under which it was gathered.

When the marriage ended, it left collateral damage in its wake.

At the time, I couldn't tell whether I refused to see what was happening or whether I was so deep inside it that leaving felt impossible. I had made vows. He was my husband. The father of my child. A man struggling with his mental health who refused to seek help. Walking away didn't feel like an option. It felt like a betrayal.

So, I stayed. I endured. I told myself this was what faithfulness looked like—that seeing things through was the same as keeping my promises.

Only later did I understand what those years had become. Unchecked mental health struggles had quietly turned into psychological and emotional abuse—damage I couldn't see until others pulled me out of it.

I was operating without a reliable internal compass. The frameworks that once organized my life—faith, marriage, permanence—had collapsed all at once. I was moving forward because I had to, not because I felt grounded. I wanted things to be better for me and my daughter. I wanted to find love again and was willing to do my part to make that happen.

When I reentered the dating world, I wasn't reckless—but I wasn't steady either. I was emotionally unarmored and rebuilding from the inside out. I was raising my daughter. Advancing my career. Reconstructing my identity and worldview after years of mental erosion I couldn't fully articulate.

I looked functional. Capable. High performing. When, in truth, I was vulnerable and unsure. I no longer trusted the compass I once relied on for the journey ahead.

So, I made assumptions. Quiet ones. Dangerous ones.

I assumed that effort meant intention.
That admiration meant care.
That chemistry was a clue instead of a warning.

I tried to treat each relationship like a separate incident. Different man. Different context. Different outcome, surely. They didn't deserve to pay for the mistakes of people in my past. But they also weren't responsible for my healing.

That's what I can see now, from this side of the desk.

These stories aren't an indictment of me or the men I dated. They're context. Clues.

Because growth isn't measured by how cleanly a story ends, but by how clearly you can see it when you finally step back and look.

The case files are open.

**Let the investigation begin.**

CASE FILE No. 01

# PROFESSIONAL HAZARD

CHARGES:

- EMOTIONAL ENTANGLEMENT
- TIMING MISFIRES
- NOSTALGIA NEGLIGENCE

CASE STATUS:

REOPENED EVERY FEW YEARS

# #01: PROFESSIONAL HAZARD

**Alias: The IT Guy**

---

**CHARGES:**

Emotional Entanglement, Timing Misfires, Nostalgia Negligence

**CASE STATUS:**

Reopened every few years

---

We met in my first "big girl" job out of college. I was married.

Driven. Climbing the corporate ladder with a tech start-up.

I'd just been tapped to lead a rapid retail launch team, and I needed a tech lead. Someone smart, fast, and flexible.

***Enter: The IT Guy***

He was talented. Sharp. Experienced. Also Married. Nerdy-handsome with piercing blue eyes and a voice so smooth it could sell secrets. He had this rogue charm, like a bad boy who had traded his motorcycle in for a company laptop.

I walked casually into his office on a Sunday afternoon wearing a ball cap and jeans. Neither of us should have been working at all. No one else was. I apologized for the interruption, looking for a good way to pitch him on joining the team. That's when I spotted the chess set on his desk.

"You play?" I asked.

He looked me over, a skeptical smirk creeping across his face.

"You? Play chess?"

I smiled, sat down and made the first move.
He had never lost. Until now.
I won more than a game that day.
I won a new friend and colleague.

I could tell he had underestimated me as a bubbly girl from sales and marketing. That wouldn't be the last time I caught him off guard. Needless to say, he joined the team. Over the next few months, we crisscrossed the country opening over twenty new stores, we became a dynamic duo. Chemistry in motion.

Late-night work sessions turned into shared dinners. Flights became long, slow conversations. We swapped music. Shared family photos. Created inside jokes. We talked about our dreams, fears, and ambitions. We were keeping it professional, but our conversations were getting deeply personal.

My husband started to notice my work stories seemed to center around these launches and the amazing adventures from the road. He even asked if there was something more between me and the IT guy. I assured him there wasn't. I had just found someone I worked extremely well with. I wasn't the cheating type. It wasn't like that.

But it got me thinking. I hadn't even noticed the chemistry building quietly beneath the surface. Until I did.

I'll never forget that one moment that changed everything.

The two of us traveling alone again, finishing a drink, winding down after another successful store launch. A pool hall somewhere in the Midwest. I don't even remember what shot I was lining up. But I do remember the look we shared when he locked eyes with me from the other end of the table.

That gaze. That pause. It was too long. Too knowing. Electric.

In an instant, the world faded. The music, the clinking glasses, the clatter of cue balls all went silent in the heat of it. We didn't touch. But we didn't have to.

I could feel it from across the room. I was overwhelmed with attraction. I could see in his eyes that he was too. This could be a serious problem for me. I had been feeling disconnected and distant from my husband for a while, but I didn't think I was susceptible to something like this. Time to sober up. Get myself together and pretend nothing happened.

Later that night, the I.T. Guy and I walked back to the hotel along the river, the moon throwing silver light on everything we weren't saying. Internally, I was frantically trying to ground myself in my reality. At one point, he stopped walking. Placed his hands on the railing on either side of me and leaned in close to me and asked,

"Are you going to act like you didn't feel that back there?"
"I thought it was just me."
"Come on. You're smarter than that."

All I could do was stare. He held my gaze intently, glancing down at my lips. Then moved in just shy of a kiss, waiting for me to move the final inch.

Caught in the grip of conflicting emotions, I found my breath and whispered, "We're married. This can't happen."

And so, it didn't. For all the right reasons.

I tossed and turned that night. How did I let this happen? Is this how infidelity creeps in? I was used to having platonic relationships with guys at work and would never consider putting my career at risk. Much less my marriage. This was a warning. An opportunity to get my heart in order, keep work at work, and focus on strengthening my marriage. I needed to put some strong boundaries in place to make sure we avoided falling into this temptation in the future.

As we settled into the flight home the next morning, I broke the tension by presenting the best thing I could think of that might anchor us back to reality and protect the professional relationship and friendship we had formed.

"When we get back, I need to meet your wife."

He blinked. I had caught him off guard again.

"Invite me over. She'll see it all over your face. She deserves to know I'm not that girl. I don't want our spouses losing trust in us over something that's never going to happen."

Within the week, they had me over for dinner. My husband declined the invitation. It didn't take long for us I to become friends too. And for a while, it worked. Boundaries reinstalled. The temptation faded and life moved on.

Then came the news: his wife cheated while he was out of town for work. Multiple times. He was wrecked. I was furious. What kind of cosmic irony is this? We had made clear choices to keep our promises, why couldn't they?

They moved to a new town to give it one more shot, but it didn't last. Patterns repeat.

She told me after they divorced that she always suspected our relationship was more intimate that we made it out to be and used that suspicion to justify her infidelity. Then she suggested that if I was ever single, he and I should revisit our connection. "There was definitely something there on his end."

I didn't let myself indulge in the suggestion, but having his attraction to me confirmed felt validating. I put it on the shelf and would revisit it anytime I was feeling unwanted or insecure.

## INSIGHT UNCOVERED

My shared attraction with the I.T. Guy caught me off guard, but in hindsight, I should have seen it coming. I thought it was safe because we were both married, but all the time spent sharing our hearts with each other opened the door. Some might even consider our close friendship an emotional affair. I didn't realize at the time, I was meeting my need for validation because home didn't offer the same warmth and connection anymore.

It was easy. Convenient. But thinking that we can invite temptation and intimacy in without consequences is a dangerous game. The more we test those boundaries, the more they fray. It only takes a moment to realize you weren't as immune as you believed yourself to be.

What I didn't fully see at the time was that I wasn't just craving his attention, I was craving who I was when I was with him. Seen. Understood. Respected. Desired. All things I had previously felt in my marriage.

> But while circumstances may cloud your judgement in the moment, and it feels so good to indulge in the chemistry and connection, at some point reality does set in. Someone else's husband isn't the answer to your search for happiness.
>
> You have to find that within yourself.

Years passed and I got divorced, due in part, to my husband's infidelity. And wouldn't you know it? My first work trip post-divorce was to the I.T. Guy's new city.

I sent the text: "I'm in town. Want to grab a drink?"

I was newly divorced and still operating without traction. The rules and religious structure that had governed my life had vanished and I hadn't yet learned what would replace them. I was functioning. I was working. But emotionally, everything was exposed.

We met at my hotel. Talked for hours. Laughed. Shared stories we hadn't told anyone else about the pain of divorce. Relived the glory days of having a great partner-in-crime at work. Reflected on the irony that it was our spouses that cheated. Admitted to our shared attraction but never regretted keeping our promises.

The wine flowed. So did the years of pent-up longing. Good thing I had packed something sexy. Just in case.

When the restaurant closed, he came up to my room. Closed the door behind him, stepping in close to me. One hand reached up to my hair, fingers curling around the back of my neck, his thumb brushing the edge of my cheek.

Looked down and held my gaze, soaking me in.

There were no spouses to hold us back now. No bosses or coworkers to give us pause. It was just us and the raw desire we had been keeping at bay for years.

And finally... he pulled me into a kiss. The world faded away all over again. This was worth the wait. My head immediately started spinning. My heart pumping. What a love story this could be.

Then just as I began to feel weak in the knees... he stopped. Pulled back. Eyes full of something between fear and tenderness.

“We can’t do this,” he whispered. “You’re not ready. It’s not right.”

I’m sorry, what?! I’m not that drunk. It’s not just me who’s been wanting this. I’m not that bad of a kisser. I am so confused! But before I could collect my thoughts and spit out my questions, he had gotten dressed, gathered his things and disappeared.

The door closed. The silence screamed. All I could do was stand in the doorway staring into the empty hallway in stunned silence. What the hell just happened? Where the hell is he going?!

I started spinning out in a tornado of confused emotion and hurt. Consumed by insecurities and distrust of my grasp on reality itself. So, I called. Too many times. Sent too many text messages. I needed answers. Surely, he owed me that much.

I’d later name that desperate, unhinged side of me “Psycho Self.”

Three days later, he finally texted: “Sorry I disappeared. I got scared. Things are too raw. I don’t want to lose you over sex.”

I didn't know whether to scream or cry. So, I chose to believe him, accept what he was saying was the truth, save the friendship, and just put things back in a box. I bandaged up my wounded ego and moved on, slowly. Eventually recognizing the mess that I was at the hotel that night. I had been desperate for it to happen. Hopeful he would be the answer to my fresh form of brokenness. That I would never have to step into the dating world at all.

## INSIGHT UNCOVERED

I always believed that once the timing was right, when we had a clear path forward, everything would fall into place for us. But what I learned that night is that timing doesn't fix fear. It doesn't erase old wounds.

When he abandoned me in that hotel room, he didn't just interrupt a moment, he shattered the story I had been telling myself about where our attraction would inevitably lead us. When my fairytale script crumbled in mere moments, I realized I was facing a much longer road than I cared to walk. It wasn't going to be that easy.

And while I tried to slip my heart back into neutral, pretend we could go back to being "just friends," the truth is once you've crossed into longing—once you've tasted the possibility of more—there's no smooth, tidy way back. Neutral isn't safe. It's just another kind of tension, stretched between what was, what is, and what will never be. And it lingers unless you give it complete closure.

In the end, I had to face a deeper truth: I wasn't reaching for him because he was my missing piece. I was reaching because I wanted to be rescued. To be reminded of the version of myself I'd been before the wreckage of divorce. But no one can rescue you from that. The work of healing, of restoration, was always mine to do. And the love I was really longing for? It had to find it within myself first.

Years passed. Our friendship survived, no thanks to Psycho Self.

One day, I was back in his city again and let him know. He invited me over. To his home this time. Told me I'd get to meet his girlfriend. And see the kids. So, I went.

And dammit. She was great.

Warm. Funny. Beautiful in that soft, resilient way. She had a tragic backstory of her own. Heartache. Trauma. A messy first marriage. They met at work, of course. They'd been dating for nearly a year.

I spent more time that day with her than I thought I would. He spent most of his time entertaining the kids. We would exchange brief glances across the room. Reminders that underneath the friendship, the attraction between us was still there.

When I stood to leave, he offered to walk me to my car. It was the first and only time we had to talk alone all day.

"Seeing you happy makes me happy," I said, "She's great. Your kids love her. You love her kids. Thanks for having me over."

We stood by the car door longer than necessary saying our goodbyes. Long enough to let the attraction surface. He brushed my hair away and pulled me in for a kiss. It was full of ache and missed opportunity.

I pulled back first. Looked him straight in the eye.

"What are you doing? As much as I'd love to tell you to hop in the car with me and give this a real shot, I need you to go inside." Then I smiled and said, "I mean, if it doesn't work out, call me."

We both laughed. We both knew I wasn't completely joking.

I drove away, a little sad, but glad for the time spent together. I felt genuinely happy for him. Secure that we'd stay friends. Hopeful that love might finally have found its way to him. Hopeful that a relationship like theirs might be right around the corner for me too. Sure enough, they got married. Another happy ending for someone I care about.

That should be the end of the story. But it wasn't.

We stayed in touch here and there over the next five years. A few phone calls. Professional references. The occasional "guy's perspective" when I was dating someone new. He always had a way of leveling me out. Encouraging me not to settle. Reminding me what I deserved. And I reminded him that he could always call me. I loved him like family. A forever friend.

Even when our numbers and addresses changed, there was always LinkedIn. We were colleagues, after all. But life moves on and check ins fade into birthday posts.

Then one day, nearly a decade later, I got a message from him: "Call me. I need you."

I immediately felt a sense of dread and concern. So, I called.

He answers the phone and it takes about 1.2 seconds for his voice to set the tone of the conversation. I had missed that voice. I couldn't wait to hear how things were going with his kids, his life on the east coast, his new business venture. But when I asked about her, his answer stopped me dead in my tracks.

"Wife?? We got divorced 2 years ago. I thought you knew. Besides, aren't you married now? You have the same guy in all your pictures."

I could hear the interest rise when I told him I was very single and the guy in the pictures was my best friend. Game on!

We laughed. Flirted. He was surprised again that I wasn't quite the strait-laced conservative Christian married woman he remembered, nor the messy divorcée he had passed on years earlier.

His marriage, the one I watched begin, was over. Messy legal battles. Custody drama. Job loss. Fractured ties. He was unraveling. He reached out in hopes of finding a soft place to land and maybe even a place to get away to. Maybe this was our time. He said he didn't want to miss another chance to be with me.

But this time, I had to be the strong one and pull back from him. I wanted to help. I offered what I could.

"I'm here. I love you. But we need to pause the flirting. Let's get you through this first. Back on your feet. Then we'll see."

He told me he loved me. Then disappeared into his crisis. Back to our pattern of sporadic texts. Occasional phone calls.

A lot of silence. His life continued to spiral out of control. I had very little information and could never seem to reach him when I wanted to check in and connect. I was trying to help but all I could do was worry.

The emotional whiplash was wearing on me, but I had made a promise: "I love you and that will never change. You can always call, no matter what. No matter how long it's been."

And I'm someone who keeps my promises. But regret and doubt about this one was starting to creep in. What is it costing me to keep making promises to people without the same desire or ability to reciprocate? Maybe it's time to take a step back, review the facts, and stop looking for evidence of love and friendship that expired a decade earlier. Maybe it's time to close this case file and walk away with a clean conscious.

## INSIGHT UNCOVERED

Sometimes we reach backward, hoping to see ourselves reflected in the eyes of someone who knew us before the wreckage. Before the heartbreaks reshaped us.

But love can't thrive on nostalgia or potential. It only survives in the messy, present-tense truth. After nearly 20 years of loyalty, I finally accepted what I'd refused to believe: I'm allowed to expect someone to show up when I call. Not just the other way around.

I used to think promises were sacred. That if I said, "you can always call," I had to mean it forever.

But some promises expire when the person on the other end stops showing up.

I wasn't holding space anymore. I was holding my breath and waiting for scraps of connection from someone I no longer truly knew. This wasn't loyalty. It was emotional self-sabotage dressed up as compassion.

You can love someone and still revoke access.
You can honor the memory and still close the case.
It's not betrayal to walk away. It's wisdom.

Maybe if I had learned that sooner, some of these other case files wouldn't exist. Then again, maybe it took a few more crime scenes to be able to identify what was happening and build the strength to distance myself from it.

# KEY WITNESS
## "Psycho Self"

**She doesn't show up often, but when she does, she's loud.**

Psycho Self is the one who dials six times in a row when someone doesn't answer. The one who fires off rapid texts, then rereads them in a panic. The one who replays the story in her head over and over and over.

**Did I say too much? Did I scare him away? Did I ruin this?**

She's the part of me that clings to validation like it's oxygen. Desperate for reassurance, terrified of abandonment, and convinced that if I just explain myself the right way, I can fix it.

**But here's the uncomfortable truth:**
Psycho Self doesn't appear because of him. She shows up because of me.

Because of the part of me that's still healing. Because of the part of me that, deep down, wonders if I'm easy to leave.

I used to hate her. I used to want to lock her away, ashamed of how needy and reckless she felt. But now? I see her for what she is: A signal flare. A mirror. A moment of vulnerability reminding me where I still need to love myself better.

**Here's the deal I've made with her:**
She's allowed to be in the car. She can even ride shotgun. But she is never, ever, ever allowed to drive—or touch my phone.

I can still feel her sometimes, gripping the wheel, yanking at the controls, the wave of anxiety rising. That's when I call a bestie in to talk her off that ledge by reminding me that I'm not crazy, just a little unhinged at the moment.

Because when I can hold Psycho Self with compassion, she quiets.

**And I remember:**
**I'm allowed to want love.**
**But I'm no longer willing to beg for it.**

# CONFESSION

## THE CHEF

### CHARGES:

Culinary seduction with a side of sudden seasonal unavailability

### WEAPON OF CHOICE:

Cast-iron confidence, tantric tenderness, and eggs over easy

# CONFESSION: THE CHEF

It had been a year since the divorce. I could feel the fog shifting and the adjustment to single motherhood settling in. Looking back, I can see that there were still a lot of open wounds driving my choices.

What haunted me most were my ex-husband's words: "I never found you attractive and no one else will either."

I couldn't unhear them. So, I did the only thing that made sense. I tested the theory. Not to prove him wrong exactly, but to see for myself what was true. I was tired of carrying shame for what I'd lost. Not just the marriage, but my confidence in what—and who—I could trust. I wasn't broken anymore. But I was disillusioned, standing amid the wreckage of promises made in the name of faith and obedience that failed to protect me.

It was time to get out there. Time to try again. Maybe even create an online profile?

I started with some basic Google searches. Found online chat rooms that helped me find my sea legs, observe, and eventually to dip a toe into flirtatious banter that had long been purged from my repertoire. I was not prepared for the "Eyes Wide Shut" experience that was waiting for me. Dark alleys filled with twists and turns, kinks and fetishes. Hedonism a la carte.

This was not safe.

But neither was saving myself for marriage and following all the rules. I no longer trusted that they could offer me a way forward. So, I clutched my sense of morality and stepped into the shadows.

A few awkward chat exchanges. A few salacious propositions denied. Then a light pierced the darkness.

He was a trained chef, tired of the restaurant industry, who had left to pursue other career opportunities in Oil & Gas.

He had been at this dating thing for a while. Knew his limits and, while charming, was upfront with what he had to offer and what he was looking for. I was taken aback by the transactional nature of his approach but appreciated the directness. I felt at ease with him, and he was more than happy to teach me a few things. So, after chatting for a couple weeks and a handful of video calls, curiosity took the keys and I accepted his invitation to spend the night at his place.

My bestie was concerned for my safety but reminded me she was just a phone call away if I needed to pull the rip cord.

The moment I stepped into his house, I noticed how every corner was well curated for him and his daughter. She was gone for the whole summer, leaving him free to focus on himself. Knowing there was no chance for anything long-term helped keep Psycho Self at bay.

Everything about him felt like meticulous care. Precise, practiced, and slow in the best way. His daily yoga practice permeated every element of his life. He moved with purpose, and his presence was both grounding and charged. What he could do with just a skillet, pot & a knife was nothing short of magical.

He was equally intense in the bedroom. Gentle but directive. Some of his requests and suggestions elicited an immediate blush but I decided to lean into the experience and let myself enjoy the education... and my first real orgasm, ever.

He made me the most mesmerizing breakfast. It was beautiful, intentional, unforgettable. Just like him.

There were no big promises made. Just chemistry, shared meals, and a quiet understanding that this wasn't built to last.

And when the summer ended, so did we.

## INSIGHT UNCOVERED

The taste of such sexual chemistry took me out of the frying pan and into the fire.

I had spent years treating desire like a liability—something to manage, confess, or suppress. Sitting across from a seasoned lover, I realized how underdeveloped my own language for pleasure had been, and how much of it I'd inherited from shame. Ideas about sex that were long past their expiration date had shaped not just what I did, but what I believed I was allowed to want.

The Chef didn't give me answers. He unlocked access. To curiosity without apology. To choice without justification. To the understanding that my body wasn't something to control or offer as proof—it was something I needed to listen to.

I had no desire to get burned. But I discovered I had an appetite for trying new things, for learning what felt good, for participating rather than performing. Pleasure stopped being evidence and became information.

I learned that some lovers feel like a season. Others, like a memory in your skin. He was both. Brief, intimate, and gone with the turn of a calendar page. I still have the French song he played me over breakfast saved in my phone.

# THE INVESTIGATION BEGINS

# 02: THE BALCONY TEST

**Alias: The Diabetic**

---

**CHARGES:**

Emotional Absence, Symbolic Illiteracy, Chronic Indifference

**CASE STATUS:**

Filed Under "Do Not Repeat"

---

Finally. A real boyfriend.

I had been enlightened beyond expectation after my dance with darkness. But I wasn't trying to take up residence in a red-light district anytime soon. I was craving something more familiar. Something well-seasoned, but maybe not quite that spicy.

***Enter: The Diabetic***

He was a clean-cut, single dad of a teenage girl. Had a good career in sales and attended the same kind of church I grew up in. And he was looking for a relationship. Bingo.

We loved to watch movies together, explore the town, listen to live music, and hang out with each other's friends. It was all so... normal. Boring even. And after all the drama of my marriage, boring was welcome. He adored my sense of adventure and well-traveled background, stating he had always wanted to travel. Maybe I had finally found my plus one! After a couple of months, I met his daughter and he met mine. He said he loved me. I said it back.

But around 90 days into the relationship, new evidence began to surface. The more I examined the scene, the more the evidence stacked up. Small details. Inconsistencies.

First, his father-daughter relationship gave me pause.

I couldn't help but notice he was available to hang out even on weekends he should have his daughter with him. When I inquired, he deflected and said she had no interest in hanging out with her boring dad. It was a teenager thing. Well, as a single mom struggling to engage a dad whose young daughter missed him all the time, I found myself quietly infuriated.

Then, there was the unmanaged diabetes.

I'm not talking about the occasional slice of cake or even a daily sweet treat. It was the flippant treatment of blood sugar drops that resulted in passing out in his car on the way to work. It was the constant stream of Diet Coke and nothing else.

Shut up, me. It's not really my business. I mean... I'm not his mom. I'm not a medical professional. It was Type 1 diabetes, and he had been dealing with it since he was a kid. I had my own weight management struggles to deal with. Surely, we could tackle our health challenges together. When I suggested we drink more water, he chuckled and said, "Diet Coke is basically water." Cue another internal side eye.

Next, pile on the disappointing intimate encounters.

It had all started out well enough. We even waited to get physical until we were well into a relationship. They say this happens to all guys sometimes, *right*? Be cool, girl. Be cool.

He was frustrated but not surprised.
"Damn diabetes. It didn't used to be like this."

Apparently, it had been an issue long enough that he had a few tools on hand that we would wind up employing early and often. Was I even allowed to complain? I'm navigating new territory here. I couldn't think of anything more cruel than to break up with someone over something so intimate. When I probed a little deeper on our options to address this long term, he was not interested in putting much effort in since his bag of tricks worked just fine for him. Okay, but what about me? Long-term? Shake it off, girl. Shake it off.

My final observation came through a work trip to Jamaica.

I didn't invite him immediately but brought it up in casual conversation hoping it would be a shared adventure.

"Do you have a passport?"
"Why would I need a passport?"
"Ummm... to be able to travel outside of the US?"
"That's never gonna happen, so why spend the money?"

Red flag.

I thought he said he wanted to travel! Clearly, I need to get more explicit on what he meant by that. Turns out the only time he had ever left the state was on a high school field trip. It may seem silly, but for someone who got her first passport at the ripe age of 4 years old, this could be a real mismatch.

Good thing I have besties ready to pack a bag at a moment's notice. Jamaica here we come.

Fast forward to our hotel balcony overlooking a pristine Caribbean beach. Morning sun, warm breeze, journal open on my lap. My best friend and co-conspirator in this escape still asleep in the room behind me. Music drifted low from my headphones, and for the first time in a while, I felt still. Whole. Safe in my own skin. It was the kind of moment that makes you believe everything's going to be alright.

Naturally, my thoughts drifted to him. My first "real" boyfriend since the divorce. Sure, there were a few mismatched things, but he was nice enough.

Then the nagging thought appeared:
I didn't miss him. I didn't wish he was there.

And when you're in a supposedly loving relationship and your soul feels lighter without them, that's not love. That's clarity.

Slow down, you. Just slow down. Before you just blow things up, we need to test the evidence. See, my marriage had left me in a position where I didn't trust my inner voice anymore. Thanks again for a bestie who was ready to process all my doubts and fears during our walks on the beach. I resolved to return home and be more observant. More critical. Use my head, not just my heart.

Before leaving Jamaica, I bought him a tailor-made souvenir. Nothing big, but a little treasure I'd picked up and carried home. Just for him.

A Jamaican Diet Coke. They call it "Coke Light" there. Perfect, right?

I handed him the bottle with childlike anticipation of his joyous reaction to this token of thoughtfulness. Not just for what it was, but what it meant. A cool keepsake that might soften him to traveling abroad. Something that said, "You were on my mind. I know you."

He twisted the cap, guzzled the drink in ten seconds flat, and tossed the bottle in the trash. Gone. No questions. No pause. No awareness of the sentiment attached to the gesture. Just like that, my intentions, my care, discarded with the recycling. No, it wasn't really about the Diet Coke. But it was absolutely about the message it carried: I see you. I choose you. You matter. And in that moment, what I saw in return was a man who didn't know how to hold what I was offering.

That's when I knew. He's a good guy. Just not my guy.

He wasn't cruel. He just wasn't curious. Not about what mattered to me. Not about what moved me. Not about me at all. He and I saw serious and humorous things much differently. He didn't do anything "wrong." But sometimes clarity doesn't need a villain. It just needs a quiet morning, a journal, and a balcony. A few days later, I ended it over the phone. I offered to see him one last time, but he declined. He didn't understand.

"You're going to miss me," he said.

Don't count on it. I didn't miss him when we were together.
I definitely didn't miss him when it was over.
I do miss that balcony.

### INSIGHT UNCOVERED

Not all crimes require a confession. Some are solved by silent observation. And when your evidence of love gets tossed in the trash, you don't need a jury to deliberate.

I didn't need another conversation. I didn't need closure. I didn't need to be understood. I needed to trust myself.

The clues our hearts and minds give us, especially when we get quiet and listen closely, won't steer us wrong. They tell us when effort isn't mutual, when desire isn't aligned, and when we're negotiating against ourselves just to keep the story going.

This was the first time I didn't do that.
Next time?
I keep the Coke Light.
I log the pattern.
And I close the file before I start rewriting the ending.

## ONE LAST SUNSET

Six months after we broke up, I saw on social media that he had gotten married. Good for him. Fast forward four years and I was surprised to see his familiar face on my Hinge feed. Divorced. Dating again.

He reached out. Said I looked beautiful. Said he didn't even remember why we broke up in the first place. Let's give it another shot. I thanked him and politely declined.

By then, I had adopted a new philosophy: no sequels. No second or third chances at something that already told you what it was the first time around. And when I say I didn't miss him, I mean it. I didn't miss the Diet Coke. I didn't miss the passport debates. I didn't miss the emotional vacancy I used to call love.

And that, my friends, is how you know you've given yourself closure. Not because it stopped hurting. But because you stopped trying to rewrite the ending. Some bottles are meant to be unopened. Some chapters, un-revisited. Some lessons fully learned.

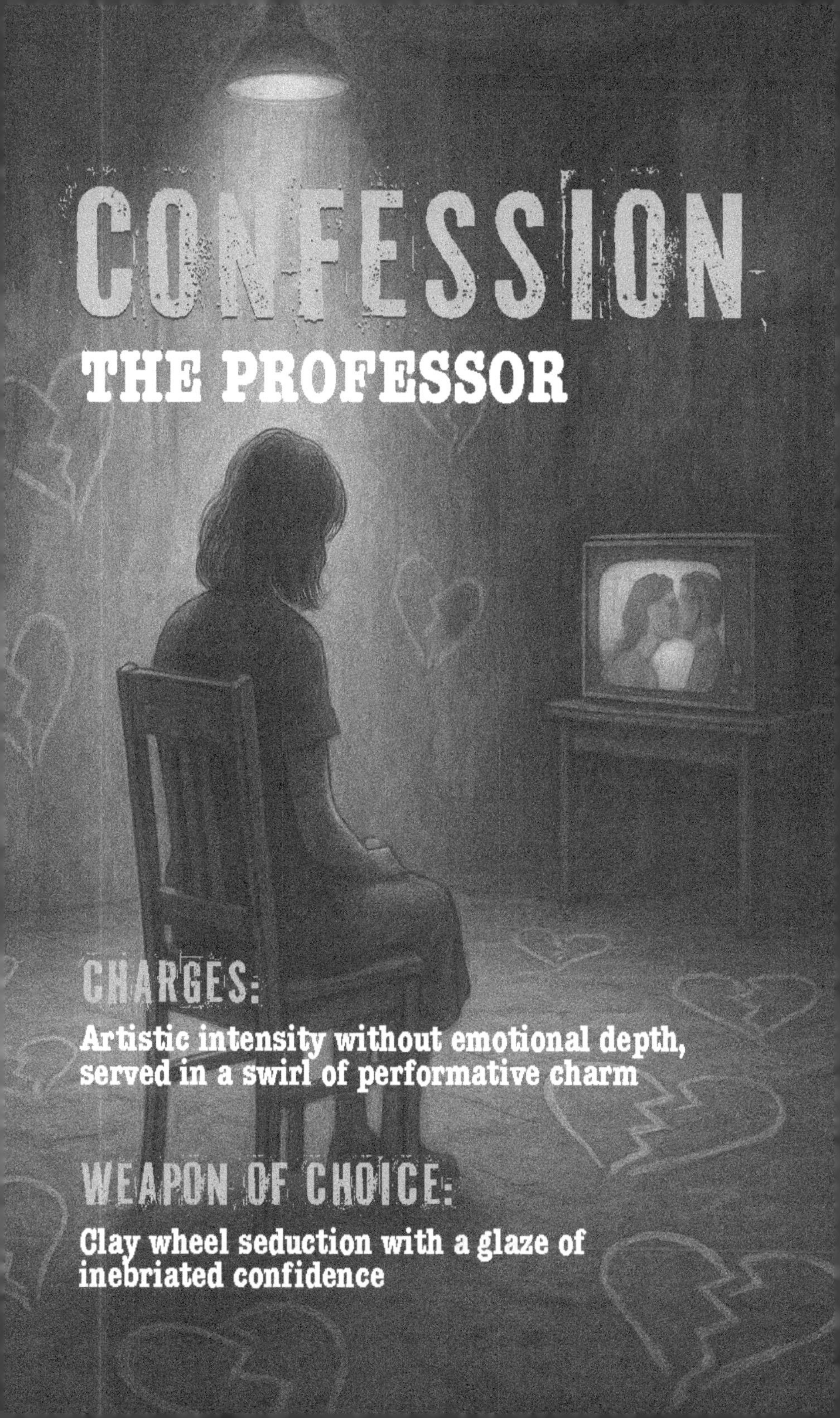

# CONFESSION

## THE PROFESSOR

**CHARGES:**

**Artistic intensity without emotional depth, served in a swirl of performative charm**

**WEAPON OF CHOICE:**

**Clay wheel seduction with a glaze of inebriated confidence**

# CONFESSION: THE PROFESSOR

Dating a professor had always held a certain allure. My parents each taught college courses. Several of my friends were professors. I had considered it as a career for myself as well. Conversations at my table often bounced between pedagogy, politics, and pop culture.

People had told me for years, "You need someone who challenges you." I agreed, but I misunderstood what that meant. I thought challenge came from credentials and clever conversation. From a man who could out-debate me or out-educate me. What I was actually hungry for was someone who would challenge my patterns. Someone who wouldn't let me carry the conversation, manage the mood, or do the emotional heavy lifting alone.

So, when his profile popped up, it felt too good to be true. Or at least it read like a well-written syllabus. Conversation flowed. His confident and articulate mind were invigorating.

As I walk into the restaurant for our first date, I spotted him immediately. Handsome. Charismatic. A well-dressed art professor.

He greets me with a strong hug and profuse flattery. Turns out he'd shown up an hour earlier and taken full advantage of the bar menu, and he was eager for me to catch up with him. He whispered in my ear that he had something amazing planned for us to do on campus after we finished our drinks. Then immediately moved in for a kiss. Bold move. A little too bold for my taste.

His liquid courage had him acting like this was our fifth date and I was the only one who thought it was the first. I was attracted, but a little put off. An hour or so later, it was time to go, but he was still drunk. I wanted to be his date, not his designated driver. We were close to campus, so I offered to drive. He leaned in for another kiss when he opened my car door. Not so fast, sir!

Then he led me to his campus art studio. A basement lined with clay wheels and half-finished sculptures. He handed me an apron, sat me at the wheel, and announced we were going to "throw some clay." Now we're talking. I've always wanted to try something like this. Anything artsy is right up my alley.

As I awkwardly fumbled with the spinning slab, he moved his stool behind me. Slowly wrapped his arms around me, hands on mine, guiding me through the motion. It was like he was attempting to recreate that scene from the movie *Ghost*. Intense. Immersive. Intimate. More than a little fast for a first date. I was able to keep things PG, slow him down a bit, keep it light and still have fun.

I genuinely enjoyed the experience. The creativity. The forethought he put into the date. So, when he asked, I agreed to meet him for lunch.

This time: No Drinks.

He spent the entire time complaining. About the town, his job, the people, the weather. Everything. I spent the entire time trying to counteract his negativity. I kept trying to move the conversation to something more optimistic or positive. I was unsuccessful.

As I smiled and nodded through lunch, it was clear it would be best to just drop this class and take an incomplete.

## INSIGHT UNCOVERED

For a long time, I thought being challenged meant being impressed. A sharp mind. Good credentials. Someone who sounded smart enough to keep up. What I learned instead was quieter.

It matters less how a man reads on paper and more how he shows up when it's just the two of you. How he carries himself. How he talks about the world. How you feel after spending an hour in his company.

Charm doesn't cover for sloppiness. And intellect doesn't cancel out a bad attitude.

I had already lived through years of heaviness, criticism, and pessimism. I wasn't interested in signing up for a lighter version of the same course.

So, I paid attention. I noticed how quickly I slipped into compensating. How tired I felt trying to redirect the conversation. How little curiosity was coming back in my direction.

That was the challenge I needed—the kind that doesn't demand effort but reveals it.

Turns out, not every professor is worth the extra credit.

CASE FILE No. 03

# SACRED GROUND

CHARGES:

- HARMONY-INDUCED HEALING
- AGE ASSUMPTIONS
- DIVINE CONFUSION

CASE STATUS:

FULL ACQUITTAL. LIFETIME ACCESS.

# 03: SACRED GROUND

**Alias: The Singer**

---

**CHARGES:**

Harmony-induced Healing. Age Assumptions. Divine Confusion.

**CASE STATUS:**

Full Acquittal. Lifetime Access.

---

A little over a year after the divorce, I went to enjoy some outdoor community theatre with a friend. She and I both knew that even after all this time had passed, I was still what you might call... walking wounded. Functional. Smiling. Showing up to life but not quite living yet.

As the sun set and the stage lights came up, I found myself fully enjoying things for the first time in a long time. At intermission, I turned to her and said, "We need to come see these every summer!" Her response was like a wake-up call.

"See them? You need to be ***in*** them! I love you, and you haven't sung at all since the divorce. God wouldn't want you to waste your gifts and talents. If you can't lead worship at church, you need to sing somewhere. Why not here?"

That's all I needed to hear. Six months later, I auditioned for the following summer season. My daughter got to participate too. She was cast in one show, I was cast in another. Finally, something to look forward to that wasn't covered in residue from the divorce. First show of the summer, I got to play mom. Get my daughter to rehearsals, work on emails from the audience while I waited. We both made new friends and had a lot of fun on stage and off.

After the final curtain call of that show, my daughter left for her annual summertime visits with family and friends. That gave me time to refuel and fully enjoy my own theatrical experience. Now, for a chorus member like me, rehearsals mean a lot of waiting on our cues from the main actors. It can be a little boring at times but also allows time to hang out with other cast members.

***Enter: The Singer***

I met him during my daughter's show, while he served as the stage manager. He made an immediate impression: Charismatic. Old soul. Quick wit. Great beard. Younger – maybe by as much as 10 years. Taking the long road, working his way through college.

While I was obviously a little older, we hit it off immediately.

I had done a lot of theatre work in high school and college, so I was more than happy to help him out backstage. Weeks of rehearsal time proved this to be a welcome friendship that arrived right on cue. The night of dress rehearsal, I'm rushing to the theatre in time to send a couple more emails, scarf down some dinner all before my call time. I find my regular spot in the audience as the theatre starts buzzing with stage crew prepping for the show. I didn't pay much attention until I saw him walk to the front of the stage for sound checks.

"One. Two. Testing. One. Two."
Five mics later and he has run out of things to say.

"Sing your favorite worship song!" The sound tech calls out.

He starts to sing, and I lose my train of thought.
He was singing ***my*** favorite worship song! Emails could wait.
His voice – and I don't say this lightly – took my breath away.

I couldn't get to him backstage fast enough.

"What was that?! I didn't know you even sang! Listen, I don't know how or when, but we're going to lead worship together someday."

He just chuckled and squinted at me with suspicion: "You sing?" I nodded and shrugged.

"Prove it."

And I did. By singing ***his*** favorite worship song. All he could do was blink.

"Freeze. Don't move." Then he sprinted away and reappeared less than two minutes later with another cast member in tow.

"Do it again."

So, I did. They just smiled at each other and said to me, "See you at church."

What just happened? Who was that guy?

Little did I know that The Singer had just been hired by a local church's music department. He was starting the Sunday after we finished the summer season. That was his new boss.

I panicked. I hadn't sung in church since the divorce.

You see, my ex-husband and I had met at church, singing. Music was at the heart of our relationship and one of the greatest casualties of its end. I had tried to sing. Tried to worship. But it was like trying to run on a sprained ankle. Even if I could, I would have to wrap it up tightly and it would still hurt like hell.

"Ok, I'll come, but no promises. I'm kind of going through something."

Time to put our budding friendship to the test with a little ugly truth. I opened up to him about my divorce. How I had been running from church, from music, from God. I wasn't in a good place. It's why I was at the theater.

He listened intently, met my pain with compassion, and finally responded, "That's okay. Run for the hills if you need to. I'll just run after you and bring you back."

I might have only known him for a month, but somehow, I believed him. I had already lost so much. So many friends. The thought of someone who wouldn't let me slip away was just what my heart needed. And just like that, we were practically inseparable the rest of the summer.

After returning from a family trip over Labor Day weekend, he came by to grab something he'd left at my house. He pointed to my piano and asked, "Do you play?" I nodded.

The sheet music was already open to ***our*** song.

"You said we'd lead worship together someday. Why not today?"

Good point, sir. I settled my nerves, sat down at the piano, and began to play. I sang. He harmonized. When we finished the song, I felt a rush. A cosmic shift in my soul.

It didn't hurt anymore.

The silence I'd carried in my chest for two years had finally broken. Something inside me had been restored. I tried not to make it a big deal of it in the moment. Breathe. Just breathe. Keep looking forward.

Then, as if he could read my mind, he said, "Did you feel that? It was like magic."

I was stunned. I wasn't crazy after all. He felt it too. So, we kept singing. Laughing. Crying. For hours. I had my voice back. My song had returned. It felt like a miracle. He felt like a miracle.

By mid-fall, we were silently dancing around our growing attachment to each other.

We both agreed that God had clearly brought us into each other's lives for a reason. Our chemistry onstage was undeniable. We matched in tone, timing, and tenderness. The joy we shared when we sang together radiated from the platform. Everyone who saw us together, especially at church, assumed we were either married or dating. Of course, we also wondered where this was going, but it felt bigger than us, and neither of us wanted to do anything to mess it up.

Why not just go with the flow? Things will happen when they are supposed to happen, right?

If this was fiction, I'd write in a juicy twist right about now.

I'd write the part where these divinely matched singers would have to face a challenge they would ultimately overcome in the name of love. Well, our plot twist came on the way to enjoy happy hour after work one day with his roommate. They met me at my office, and we headed to the restaurant together.

Tapas and live music. My favorite.

"You think we'll get in?" his roommate asks.

"Yeah, they don't check IDs until after 7pm," the Singer replies.

Did he just say IDs?!

My entire body went still. My mind races to put together missing clues to explain that exchange. My stomach drops. I just have one question.

"Wait… what direction does your driver's license face?"

He blinked and said, "I'll be 21 in two months. Why?"

I nearly wrecked the car. Over the last four months, we never talked about our ages. Not once. Sure, there was a clear age difference. But this?

"TWENTY-ONE?!" I exclaimed. He laughed, then squinted.

"Wait! How old are you? Thirty? Twenty-nine? I know you're older, but what's ten years?"

"I'm thirty-eight."

Silence.
Then laughter.
Then a whole new understanding.

Time to do some soul-searching. We knew we never wanted to stop singing together, but were we even allowed to entertain the idea of more? Age was just a number. But 18 years? We decided to keep that bit of evidence to ourselves while we sorted out our feelings for each other and tried to figure out what this really was. Our relationship felt divine, and after much consideration and confessing our mutual attraction, we agreed not to pursue anything romantic. We would just let this be whatever it was meant to be. No labels. No agenda. Just enjoy our deepening friendship.

While I had never met anyone like The Singer, elements of our friendship felt very familiar.

Our relationship was reminiscent of the connection I had with my ex-husband before we started dating and eventually got married. The depth of our conversation was similar, the musical chemistry was undeniable, and the public pressure to pursue a romantic partnership was just as strong. At times, I had contemplated the parallel universe that might have existed had I just remained friends instead of getting married. But he and I both believed that we were supposed to get married. We were supposed to pay attention to people in the church. We were supposed to follow the cosmic signs from God that told us to be together. Those were the rules. But I wasn't in college anymore. I had seen where following that path led. I had trusted the signs, instead of questioning my own heart.

Could I just be friends with a man without an external boundary like work or marriage to keep us from crossing the line? Could I let go of the deeply held construct of how things should go according to the rules?

Fortunately, the Singer and I were on the same page. The age difference slowed us down. The fact that I was a single parent slowed us down. But we were rewriting the rules together and enjoying the adventure of it all.

With him, I had the chance to do things differently. He was my "cosmic redo."

So, when I needed a plus one on a trip to Mexico eight months later, he seemed like the best and obvious choice.

The trip was epic. Where my ex and I would have already gotten into a dozen fights, he and I were sailing effortlessly through every travel frustration. My fatal mistake was attempting to keep up with this newly 21-year-old at the bar. Hey, it seemed like a great idea at the time. We had a blast, and despite our decision to keep things platonic, we found ourselves kissing.

And the next morning? He acted as if nothing had happened. I wasn't about to ruin the trip, so I held it in for days as he nursed his hangover and I tried to hold Psycho Self at bay. I just smiled. Laughed. Pretended. Until the plane ride home, when he insisted on taking the window seat. Who does this kid think he is? I sat fuming in the middle seat until take off. Then I finally lost it.

"Hey! Are you really going to just kiss me then act like nothing happened?"

His face fell. He stared at me like a deer in headlights while he tried to understand what I just asked him.

"No. Oh my god. I'm so sorry. What?! I don't remember anything about that night at all. Why didn't you say anything sooner?"

Hold up. I needed to recalculate. As someone who had never experienced a hangover or memory loss when I drank, I never considered the possibility of him forgetting. Did Psycho Self just rob me of my ability to enjoy the last couple days in paradise?

Ok, detective. How are you going to handle this one? Lock him up and throw away the key? Put him under the piercing bright light of interrogation and break his spirit for not handling this better? Or is it you that needs to settle down and give him the benefit of the doubt?

So… we talked. A lot. We worked through it. The whole trip home. By the time we landed, we committed to something we now call "extreme honesty." Because what we had wasn't fragile. It was rare and we were determined to protect it.

The public pressure for us to date us didn't go away. The pressure to follow the scripted path didn't go away.

"You two are perfect together."

"Have you seen yourselves onstage?"

"Just admit you're in love."

We would reinforce our decision to just be friends and lean on the age difference to deflect. Meanwhile, I pouted privately. We commiserated occasionally. We called it "The 5%." Ninety-five percent of me was content being friends. But that stubborn 5%? It wanted more. It continued to question – what's missing here? Why not him? If anyone can work this out it would be us!

Finally, I landed on a hunch. A possible lead that I was hoping didn't go anywhere. But I had to know.

One night after church, during one of our deep chats, I finally asked, "Are you gay?"

He recoiled. He was shocked at the question. I had offended him.

"No! Why would you think that?"

I laughed a little.

"I mean, you're an opera singer. You do musical theatre. You've really never been asked that question before?"

At first, he bristled. Eventually, he softened. Finally, he let me in. He admitted he had questioned things. He had even experimented a little. But he worked at the kind of church where being openly gay could cost him everything. Even the judgment and presumption of others had already cost him dearly. He had gone to great lengths to avoid the issue altogether, obey the rules, and be a good example of faith.

"It's not what I want," he said. "It's not what God wants."

"I want to have a family."

We sat in silence. In complete understanding.

Another level of our friendship unlocked.

He took the risk that I could handle his full vulnerability. Little did he know his struggle would resonate with me more deeply than I expected.

I'd once believed as so many do: that being gay was incompatible with faith. That it was an irreconcilable sin. That love had limits. While my understanding was limited and my previous stance on this issue had cost me friendships earlier in life, something about what he said resonated. I had said similar words just a few years earlier about my marriage ending.

***"It's not what I want. It's not what God wants. What about our family?"***

I had made every effort to stay on the straight and narrow road: attending church, avoiding temptation, reading the bible, protecting my virginity, and volunteering for countless bible studies, mission trips and special events. By all accounts, I had done everything "right."

And still, I had been betrayed. Abandoned. Crushed. Ashamed. Divorce had completely shattered my spiritual and religious certainty.

I knew what it felt like to lose your faith and find it again in pieces.

To sit in shame and ask if you were still lovable to God.

What am I supposed to say now? I had learned the hard way that this was not the moment to quote scripture at him or lure him into my spiritual confusion. This issue was as deeply personal to him as my healing journey around my sexuality was to me. I searched my heart for the right thing to say, for what felt like forever.

Finally, I broke the silence and said,

"Listen. It matters but it doesn't matter to me. Here's where I'm at… Ignore the people who say you have to be gay. Ignore the people who say you can't be. Ignore the shame that threatens your courage. This is between you and God. You and the mirror. I'm prepared to stand still with you until you tell me which way we are going."

That moment changed everything.
Not because he suddenly knew who he was.
But because he knew he didn't have to know it alone.
I could feel a familiar rush come over me. Just like that first time we sang at my piano.

Our friendship had become sacred ground.

### INSIGHT UNCOVERED

While some love stories don't follow the script, they can lead to a happy ending all their own. Every spark doesn't need to lead to romance. Some may lead to a different kind of love and acceptance.

It was through complete acceptance that I found the safety I needed to face hard questions without the pressure of having all the answers. I found the patience to reflect on all the "what ifs" of my decision to get married. I found my footing and my faith again.

Our friendship facilitated healing for one another without having to do or say anything on anyone else's timeline. All that was necessary was heartfelt honesty and the courage to be vulnerable. What felt like frailty at first became formative in my journey forward.

Thanks to this young singer, I began to trust my inner voice and was able to share my gifts with others.

He's a keeper. A best friend for life.

## ANSWERED PRAYER

Spoiler alert: He is gay and happily married to a man I adore. He loves God more authentically than most people I've ever known.

Over the last decade, we have sat front row for every season of each other's lives. It took him a few more years to reconcile his sexuality, and a few more still to land in a professional space where he could live it safely and authentically. Through it all, we remained fiercely committed to our friendship.

He's been my best plus-one to weddings, events, and seasons that called for both laughter and courage.

He is, without exaggeration, my gay soulmate. My daughter calls him her "guncle." His mom and twin sister? They're family now. Not by blood, but by bond.

Anytime I start to run for the hills or either of us edges toward our old, self-sabotaging patterns, we show up for each other. We remind each other who we are. What we deserve. What's worth holding onto. What's worth believing.

It's a powerful thing to know that you are having just as profound an effect on someone else as they are having on you. Not by doing anything special, but by showing up exactly as you are.

He remains my favorite person to sing with. Worship partners until the end. When my mother passed and my dad asked me to sing at her service, I knew I couldn't do it alone. He was there by my side without hesitation. In perfect harmony.

In a world full of half-hearted connections and complicated endings, he is proof that sometimes – even when things don't work out the way we originally envisioned – they can turn out better than we ever imagined.

**Case File: Permanently Open.**

CASE FILE No. 04

# THE BUNGALOW OPTION

CHARGES:

- GRAND THEFT FANTASY
- EMOTIONAL TRESPASSING
- REPEAT OFFENDER

CASE STATUS:

SEALED. NO VISITATION. NO APPEALS.

# 04: THE BUNGALOW OPTION

**Alias: The Painter**

---

**CHARGES:**

Grand Theft Fantasy, Emotional Trespassing, Repeat Offender

**CASE STATUS:**

Sealed. No Visitation. No Appeals.

---

After everything with The Singer, I finally felt whole again. Stronger, more grounded, and ready to try dating with a clear head and an open heart. But the bar had been reset. I had tasted real connection, emotional presence, and spiritual intimacy. That wouldn't be easy to replace.

Still, I wasn't thrilled about returning to the world of online dating. Swiping felt tedious. Profiles were a blur. The apps felt more like vending machines of disappointment than pathways to connection. Still, I had made a quiet decision: I was ready to try.

Turns out I never had to set up a profile.

***Enter: The Painter***

It was a simple DM. Just another high school classmate reconnecting on Facebook. Nothing different than I had done with many people before. I didn't remember a lot from high school, but I enjoyed revisiting those years through other people's stories. Turns out, he had moved before we graduated but had been reconnected through our recent reunion committee efforts.

He remembered everything. Especially about me.

"You were the Colonel's daughter. Smart. Beautiful. Popular. Untouchable."

I remember thinking he must have me confused with someone else. Smart, sure. But beautiful? Popular? Not hardly. There were no homecoming courts for me. No football team boyfriends. Hardly any boyfriends at all, as a matter of fact. I was wrapped up in my grades, playing clarinet in the band, choir, theatre, church, and a variety of unsung clubs focused on community service or academics. Yet the way he remembered me? I wanted to see myself through his eyes.

He didn't see my insecurities or failures. All he saw was someone beautiful, accomplished, a good mom, and best of all... sexy. After years of being told I wasn't attractive, wasn't desirable, wasn't enough, I let myself believe him.

Go ahead, sir. Please say more.

When we talked, hours slipped by unnoticed. We had decades to catch up on. I was drawn to his story. The road he had walked. The things he had overcome. He had survived abandonment and loss. He had faced a life of instability and found a way forward. He had built his life with very little support and wasn't proud of all of the roads he had walked down. But he never lost hope, found his faith, and was actively repairing his relationship with his kids after moving across country to be closer to them. The broken road I had walked helped me resonate with the redemption I heard in his story.

He was artistic and endlessly creative, always sketching out new ideas, repainting a room, and dreaming up ways to make something better. There was an intensity to him. Raw, expressive, and unfiltered.

He lived on the other side of Texas, so at first, I didn't seriously consider dating him. The distance alone felt impractical. Our lives weren't similar either. He was a freelance commercial painter. I was firmly planted in the corporate world.

But this was his shot with his high school dream girl.
And he was going to take it.

## PART ONE: DREAM COME TRUE

Weeks of long phone calls gave us plenty of time to build the attraction. He didn't shy away from describing his fantasies and desires. It wasn't long before talking turned into planning. Before I had time to second guess myself, or him, we had coordinated a visit.

The chemistry was instant. Physical. Emotional. Consuming. He adored me. Worshiped me. We lost ourselves in each other. For hours. Days, even. I had never experienced desire that felt so raw, so affirming. It was intoxicating.

We started seeing each other about once a month. His town. My town. Somewhere in the middle. Only when my daughter was away. Only when I could set everything in my life aside and step into our bubble.

Inside that bubble, time froze. We suspended our flaws, our facts, and our futures. It wasn't sustainable, but it was addictive. I was hooked.

He wanted to take care of me. In more ways than one. Over time, he started bringing his tools to fix things around the house. Offering to help in any way that made my life just a little bit easier. A part of me loved the idea that I could help him, too. That together, we might create something from what others had broken.

Looking back, this wasn't naïveté. It was timing. I had grown a lot and knew what I wanted, but I wasn't practiced yet at choosing differently. I wasn't just drawn to him. I was drawn to the feeling of being needed. He wasn't just a project guy. He was the project. There was a part of me that wanted to be his redemption story. That was my first mistake: confusing purpose with partnership.

When he came to town, my house became our bungalow. A beautiful retreat for just us, indulging the fantasy. Anytime we were together and conflict started; we solved it with sex. Everything else just faded away. Weekend visits started stretching into weeks while the kids were away in the summer. I started getting used to having someone regularly around to share the load. So, when it was time for me to leave for a family vacation to Disneyworld to celebrate my parent's 50$^{th}$ wedding anniversary, I trusted him completely to look after everything in my absence. It seemed like a perfect solution. We would miss each other, but he assured me I had nothing to worry about. I had no way to anticipate that the distance would have such a dramatic effect on him.

Between the time difference and the vacation activities, I would only have a chance to connect with him right before bedtime, and text messages were infrequent during the day. After our first full day of family adventure, I was met with ten missed calls from him along with voicemails and text messages. Each filled with increasing agitation. When I finally returned his calls, I was met with a blast of drunken anger and accusation.

"Where have you been? Why are you ignoring me? I love you so much, but you don't even care."

This was no longer a fairytale.

It turns out that while I was away, he entertained himself by exploring the local bar scene. The next day a friend texted me to inform me that they saw him leave a bar the night before very drunk, driving my car. Excuse me?

This fantasy was going dark.

When I got home and had more time to discuss what happened with him, he was incredibly apologetic. I was furious. How dare he act the fool in a town where I had a professional reputation to protect? How dare he drive my car—any car—after drinking too much? How dare he invade my family vacation with baseless accusations? How could I put my trust in him after this? The truth was, I couldn't. The problem was, I was hooked. Attached. He offered intensity, utility, and a kind of admiration I'd never experienced. How was I supposed to let that go? I ignored my own instincts in favor of the potential I saw in him and the story I wanted to write for us both.

We weren't building a life together; we were building a hideout.

He spent the next couple of weeks proving his love for me, including getting a tattoo in my honor after I encouraged him not to go that far. He brought me back to the bubble and promised it would never happen again. And it didn't. For months. In that time, I had struggled to let him into my social life. I leaned on The Singer for plus ones to community events and work parties. My Painter was best suited for the bungalow.

It wasn't fair but it was how I felt.

He said he didn't mind, but the night before my first public speaking gig ever, he showed his true colors. I had gone to bed early to get a good night's sleep. He had decided to go out.

After last call, he came straight home to clear the air. Jolting me awake, I sat in a sleepy stupor listening to him rage about how I was neglectful and selfish. How he felt betrayed and deserved to be treated better. How he would never be good enough for me. I begged him to talk about this when I got home from work the next day. I needed to sleep. But no.

He raged until sunrise.

I quickly compartmentalized, switched gears and went to work. When I got back, while I was still in work-mode, I ended it. I was not going to tolerate his unhinged tirades, and I was not going to allow this pattern to play out in front of my daughter.

The breakup was filled with as much passion as other parts of our relationship. Texts, social media, voicemails. All filled with varying tones from vicious to repentant. I no longer felt safe with him. I needed a way to detox from this addiction.

So, when the fighting stopped, I went silent. Full radio silence.

Case sealed. Bubble burst. Fantasy revoked.

### INSIGHT UNCOVERED

Desire is flattering. Being someone's fantasy feels powerful—healing even—until you realize you're not being loved, you're being consumed. You're no longer a partner. You're a projection.

He saw me through an idealized lens—a version of me that never really existed. And after years of feeling undesirable, I leaned into his vision. What took me longer to see was that I was doing the same thing. I wasn't loving him for who he was. I was loving the man he might become.

I treated potential like proof. I believed effort and intention could outweigh pattern and instability. The danger of potential is that it keeps you loyal to a future that only exists if you keep ignoring the present.

I wasn't as healed from my divorce as I believed. I was still integrating the lessons. So, when familiar chaos showed up dressed as devotion and grand gestures, I didn't question it. I tolerated it. I turned it into something it wasn't.

# PART TWO: THE FAMILY PORTRAIT

I told myself I'd learned my lesson. That I'd closed the door for good. But some stories don't stay in their file. Some offenders return to the scene. What I didn't know then was that this case wasn't over. Not even close.

Nine months of silence went by.

By then, dating had started to feel like a chore. I knew what was out there. I'd seen enough profiles, enough patterns. I was tired of false starts and premature emotional labor. Tired of explaining myself. Tired of auditioning for connection.

My daughter and I were grounded again—just the two of us. Healthy. Busy with community theatre and family activities. Life felt steady.

So, when I got a follow request on Instagram from the Painter, I clocked it as harmless. He said he had stopped drinking. Said he wasn't trying to get back together. Just wanted to be friends.

Friends. Sure. Let's be friends.

That worked just fine until he showed up unannounced, after driving seven hours to my house, on Thanksgiving Day.

With flowers.
And an engagement ring.

A lifetime of watching romantic comedies had taught me to recognize a grand gesture when I saw one. This was his. Standing there in my open garage. Thick with anticipation.

His eyes glimmered, searching mine for an uncontrollable recognition of his love for me and validation that we were never meant to be 'just friends.' We were meant to prove that a fantasy like ours could be reality. I was supposed to be overcome with love and gratitude at his effort. All I felt was fury. Where he saw devotion, I saw someone who had acted on impulse without any consideration for where I would be or what I would be doing. He was there to get what he needed. To be put first before anything else that mattered to me. Not other commitments. Not family. Not boundaries I had clearly set.

I didn't trust myself to respond honestly in that moment. It was late. My family was expecting me for dinner. It felt cruel to send him back on the road. So, I did what I always did when I wasn't ready to decide. I delayed.

I gave him a time and place later that day and agreed to talk. We were friends, after all. Hours later, I headed to a neighborhood park to straighten things out. He had time to reflect before I arrived. He explained how he could understand why I didn't love his surprise. But his heart was in the right place. His heart was with me and would always be.

"I'm sober. I'm back in church. Let's build something real. I know you love me."

I let him talk. Let him show me the ring again. Hug me. Kiss me. Something about his touch could instantly short circuit my entire nervous system. My higher self and better judgment were inaccessible. Chemistry flooded in, intoxicated me all over again, and all I wanted was our bubble.

Maybe this time will be different
Maybe I just need to let him in.
Maybe this is what choosing healthy actually looks like.

Round two with the Painter didn't stay in the bungalow. This time, it came with kids, church, dinner tables, and birthday parties. Real life. He met my family and friends. I met his youngest two children.

Everyone was thrilled. Everyone but me. What is wrong with me?

I finally have a man willing to cross the entire state of Texas for me and it's not enough? I finally have a man skilled around the house and in the bedroom and it's not enough? I finally have a man that fell in love with both me and my daughter and it's not enough? Get with the program.

The hardest part was my difficulty connecting with his children. I'm not proud to admit it even now. I couldn't imagine being their stepmom. My daughter loved her potential new siblings and being the older sister. They were never happier than when we were all together as a family. But occasionally I would catch myself disconnecting. I would be on the outside looking in. This wasn't Psycho Self. This was something quieter. Heavier. This was me watching the fantasy fade, and I didn't fit into the reality.

Time to call the besties. The best partners a detective can turn to when she is too close to the evidence. They didn't rush me. They listened. Offered support and understanding. Then challenged me to take a long, hard look at all the evidence again. Evidence I had been ignoring since the beginning.

His pattern of emotional instability had been minimized without the drinking, but it would still rear its ugly head on occasion. His kids, all five of them, had faced chronic instability thanks, in part, to broken homes and years of delinquent child support. Details I neglected to ask about because I wasn't prepared to hear the potential truth of his financial instability. His smoking habits went against my established list of non-negotiables and were setting a negative example for my daughter. Everywhere I looked, I saw another example of how I was compromising myself to feel the warmth of his admiration and electricity of his touch.

The glare of the hot white light that those friends helped shine on the situation became blinding. They weren't interrogating me. They weren't accusing or judging me, but they weren't going to let me off the hook either. They were going to keep me honest. They were not going to hold back the truth of where my own compromises had brought me.

It was time to face it. I wanted the fantasy, not the family. I wanted the bungalow option.

I wanted to pause my real life and responsibilities every couple of months to escape into a place where the truth didn't matter—only the high that happened when we were alone together. How hard could that be? All we needed to do was find a little place somewhere. Preferably with trees and water nearby. No cell service. With a comfortable bed and a well-stocked fridge, we would have all we needed for a few days. Then we could go back to reality.

The realization of my motives exposed what I was hiding from myself and hiding from him. I was afraid I would hurt him, lose him, or worse — be painted as the villain in this story. He may have been a disaster, but at least his motives were pure. He wanted it all. He wanted me. The whole package. All I wanted was a fix. As time went by it became harder to hide my inner conflict. His life was finally coming together for him, while mine was quietly unraveling. I didn't have the courage to confront him and go through another messy break up after last time. So, I just kept it inside and played along until I couldn't anymore.

My facade finally shattered one night after the kids went to bed, snuggled up on the couch together watching a movie. He paused the TV, kissed me, and went on to describe, in vivid detail, the joy-filled future he envisioned for us. The moment in time where we were living all together, full custody of all the kids, dogs, a yard, and of course, our family portrait hanging on the wall.

Us. The kids. A forever.
Everything was coming together perfectly.
Everything I said I ever wanted.

As I visualized the family portrait, my body recoiled. Nausea. Tightness. Full-body rejection that I could not ignore.

This wasn't about coming clean with him. This was a wake-up call for me to face the truth of what I wanted and what I didn't. No more procrastinating.

I anticipated his reaction and knew he wouldn't take it well. He would feel like this was coming out of nowhere. That this time he had done everything "right" and it didn't matter. He would call me a liar. Blame me for ruining a good thing. Something in me felt like I deserved whatever response he might have, no matter how hurtful. Since I was ending it, it was my job to face the consequences, ride out the storm, and move forward. I underestimated everything. I never expected him to escalate things.

He started drinking again. The old toxic cycle was back in full force. I did my best to deflect the angry tirades and avoid getting baited into arguments. Nothing seemed to diffuse the situation.

One night, after I refused to answer the door and ignored multiple phone calls and text messages, he sat in my driveway for hours past midnight. I silenced everything and found a way to sleep through it. My daughter, 12 years old at the time, did not. I found out the next day that he had pounded on the door a few more times throughout the night, waking her up. She had gone outside to talk to him and calm him down. She had done the same thing with her dad. She tried to get the Painter to see that he was making everything worse. She pleaded for him to leave before he woke me up. Before I could call the authorities and she would lose him for good.

Hearing what happened, I was appalled. That was the line and he crossed it for the last time. Shame hit me hard. I was embarrassed. I had brought this on myself. I had invited this into my house. Into my daughter's life. Right as we were finally feeling healthy again.

It was time to lock the door and throw away the key. Time to choose my needs and my truth over someone else's happy ending at my expense.

## INSIGHT UNCOVERED

When you say you want one thing but recoil when it's offered, the problem isn't the offer. It's the part of you that already knows the ending and isn't ready to say it out loud. I wasn't avoiding commitment. I was avoiding clarity and the confrontation it would require.

I never truly saw a future with him. Not the kind built on shared responsibility, daylight decisions, and years that demand more than chemistry. Admitting that would have required me to admit another failure. Another example where hope didn't pan out. Another story I couldn't fix by trying harder.

So, I delayed. I muted my instincts. I stayed just long enough to keep the fantasy alive and my hands clean. I told myself I was being kind, patient, reasonable, when in truth, I was postponing grief and disappointment.

I didn't miss the warning signs. I ignored them because acknowledging them would have required me to stop chasing the thing that kept me afloat: the fantasy, the chemistry, and the relief of being wanted without being fully accountable. By this point in my journey, I could recognize misalignment. I just didn't always act on it. Unfortunately, choosing not to decide is still a decision—with consequences.

The moment my daughter stepped into a situation I had rationalized, delayed, and minimized was the point of no return. Not because she was harmed, but because she had to be braver than I was. She carried weight that was never hers to hold.

From that moment on, something shifted. I could survive disappointment. I could survive being misunderstood. But I would never again survive betraying my commitment to raising my daughter in a safe and healthy environment.

# PART THREE: BREAKING THE SPELL

In the months after our second collapse, I changed jobs. I tried dating again. A few new names. Fewer new sparks. Nothing that held. By the time the Painter resurfaced, I wasn't longing for him. I was just weary of ghost towns and dead ends. Tired of believing there was someone out there who might actually show up and stay.

So, when the message came through unexpectedly from an unknown number in Alaska, I didn't delete it. It was the Painter.

He said he'd changed. That part felt familiar. Said he wanted to prove himself and earn my trust.

And I, now a little older, a little lonelier, still craving something solid, gave in to Psycho Self's incessant pleading to reply. She insisted that we accept his compliments and affection again. We are starving for attention and affirmation, after all. No need to pretend we were destined for each other or paint over the past. No need to give him unfettered access to our life. Just see where this goes. It'll be okay. We'll be fine.

Not so fast, Psycho Self. I would respond to his text, but make things clear from the start:

"I don't believe this will work. We've tried. We have a pattern. An intoxicating, destructive, impossible-to-ignore loop. Neither of us has been strong enough to stay out of it."

I reminded him how we always started hot. Always slid into comfort. Always mistook adrenaline for love and admiration for stability. I told him I was open to friendship from afar. I would still be dating other people.

"You want the family portrait. I only ever wanted the bungalow. That should be enough of a red flag to make you run."

I meant it. And somehow, I also believed I could manage it.

But he didn't run. He said he was stronger now. More grounded. Ready to break the cycle. I made him a promise: at the first sign of the pattern returning, the smallest whiff of old habits, it was over. No drama. No debate. Just done.

He agreed.

He was living in Alaska, working hard labor in impossible cold. But since his kids were in Texas, that meant he'd be back often. Summers. Holidays. Spring Break. Distance felt like protection. Like control.

"Next time I'm close, I want to see you," he said. I told myself that it was fine.

Boundaries were clearly stated. History had been aired like evidence in court. This time, we knew better. I wouldn't let myself get too deep.

New Year's Eve came around. I met him in Dallas, a safe distance from my home life. I booked the hotel. He brought the wine. And with just a single embrace, I was back in the bungalow. My favorite place to hide. A place where I could have intensity without alignment. Desire without consequence. Where my body could feel chosen without my life needing to agree.

The way he looked at me. The way he touched me. Like he still believed we were inevitable. That night was magic. Not because it was perfect. Because it was familiar. And familiarity had always known how to dress itself up as fate. I told myself it was a holiday exception. A controlled burn. But when the sun came up, I was still under the spell. So was he.

I hadn't exited the pattern. I had just found a quieter way back into it.

He followed up our New Year's tryst with all the right moves. Regular texts. Midday check-ins. Flowers for no reason. A Valentine's Day gift that felt thoughtful. I'll admit it. I was surprised. Even a little impressed. It looked like maybe, just maybe, we could break the pattern.

Spring Break was approaching quickly. He was visiting his kids, and we planned time together after. I arranged my schedule to match his dates and caught myself looking forward to it.

Hope crept in, wearing heels and red lipstick. Maybe this was our third act miracle.

But I was worried. Worried enough to bring it up in therapy. I was doubting his capacity to see this through. I was doubting my ability to hold my ground. I had hoped therapy would talk me out of my fears. Help me see the good and press forward with optimism. Instead, my therapist confirmed them.

She pointed out that my upbringing gave me stability. That trauma had caused insecurity and mistrust in my life, but despite my desire to empathize with the Painter's experiences, his upbringing was rooted in instability. I embodied stability for him, but he didn't have the capacity to offer the same in return.

She said, "There are not enough years in this lifetime for him to do the work necessary to catch up to your sense of stability and self-assurance."

She was right. I heard her. And still, I wasn't ready to let him go. I was already attached and entangled in what we had together, not what we had become. I would choose to proceed with caution. Keep my wits about me.

Unexpected delays to his trip didn't help with my worry. With each delay, no matter the reason, hope shrank back into the shadows, arms crossed, muttering "I told you so."

But then, he showed up. He was determined to prove me wrong. Two weeks in Texas. One with his kids. One with me. We made every effort to start out with a clean slate.

A few days into his visit, I walked into my house after work to find his birthday gift to me.

A new light fixture for the kitchen that he had installed while I was gone that day. It was beautiful, oversized, expensive — and completely wrong for the space. He was so proud. I had been complaining about my light fixture for years but never prioritized it in the budget. He had taken those comments and decided to take care of it for me. Another grand gesture. Another solution I hadn't asked for.

I scrambled to control my expression and find the perfect response. I couldn't help but wonder how he could even afford it, and why my discomfort always arrived after the gesture, never before. I felt awful. Not awful enough to leave it there. He was crushed when I said I wanted him to uninstall it and return it. I reassured him that I recognized the effort. I understood the message he was trying to send. I was grateful. We did our best to clear the air before he left town, but I had killed the mood.

When the credit card statement arrived with a charge from the local lighting store, I was incensed. He couldn't afford it after all. I searched for a return or a refund. Nothing. I couldn't believe he still had access to the credit card I let him use to fix the fence all those years ago and I had forgotten. I couldn't afford this.

Another flashback. Another moment where generosity was funded by me. Another reminder that intensity can feel like care while quietly eroding trust and inviting shame. I could no longer afford to go on. He had stolen from me. Lied to me. I had already called to verify the purchase and lack of return. When I called to confront him, he denied it. Said he was going to cover the cost of it, and he was just getting me credit card points. He would pay me back.

But I was done. Not because this was the worst thing he had done, but because it was the clearest. I had forgiven bigger things. Overlooked louder warnings. But this was small. Ordinary. Out of place. Like the wrong fixture in a familiar room, it finally made the misalignment between us impossible to ignore.

Despite his objections, I made it clear for the last time that I was done.

***"I am no longer willing to make the sacrifices required to make this relationship work."***

As those words left my mouth, I felt restored to truth.
No more justifying. No more bargaining. No more bungalow.

The spell had been broken. I wasn't the girl in his portrait. And I was finally okay with that. It was time to pause, step back, and find a vision I truly wanted to frame my life around.

That was the last time we spoke.

## INSIGHT UNCOVERED

Some love stories aren't meant to be lived. They're meant to be survived.

I didn't keep going back because I didn't know better. I kept going back because the relationship let me stay in intensity without alignment. I could feel chosen without being known. Desired without being considered. Alive without having to integrate that feeling into my real life.

I knew it wasn't right. I knew it wasn't forever. And still, attachment is persuasive. From that place, I justified what should have been questioned. I softened boundaries. I explained away patterns. I muted clarity so I wouldn't have to let go of something that felt good, even when it wasn't good for me.

It wasn't the biggest betrayal that stopped me. It was the clearest one.

A simple, out of place light fixture illuminated what didn't fit in my life. It wasn't just wrong for the room. It was wrong for me. And once I saw that misalignment, I couldn't unsee it.

This case taught me that awareness isn't the same as readiness. Love doesn't cancel patterns. Chemistry doesn't fix instability. And intensity can keep you loyal long after something stops being safe, sustainable, or true.

What mattered wasn't how many times I could have ended it. What mattered was that something finally cut through the fog. That final moment of clarity didn't make me wiser. It made me stronger.

I finally chose accountability over attachment. Alignment over adrenaline. I started building a life I didn't want to escape from.

So, I stopped dating. I got quiet. I listened. And I wrote what I needed next.

**The Dating Manifesto.**

Not rules. Not resolutions. A declaration – shaped by evidence, boundaries, and hard-won clarity. Because sometimes closure doesn't come from another conversation. It comes from deciding what you will no longer negotiate.

# DATING MANIFESTO

Sometimes it takes dozens of dates, a few heartbreaks, and a lot of reflection to realize that the clearest truths were there all along. This manifesto isn't about blame. It's about clarity. These are the truths I've gathered, earned, and etched into my bones. Let them be reminders, not rules. Anchors, not armor.

1. **People will tell you who they are.** Believe them.
2. **Closure is a gift you give yourself.** Stop waiting for someone else to deliver it.
3. **Avoid all sequels.** The reasons it ended are still reasons.
4. **Consistency > Chemistry.** Sparks fade. Patterns don't lie.
5. **Love is not a project.** You can't build someone into being ready.
6. **You are not intimidating.** You are clear. That's their discomfort to manage.
7. **Peace is the proof.** If your nervous system doesn't trust them, neither should you.
8. **Timing isn't everything, but it's a lot.** Aligned hearts still need aligned calendars.
9. **How they talk about their exes is how they'll talk about you.** Listen carefully.
10. **Not every story needs a romantic ending.** Close the case or re-categorize. Unfinished business doesn't need to linger.
11. **Drama belongs on a stage.** Stirring up conflict only wastes time. Focus on your part in it and what you can control.
12. **It's about you, not them.** Be radically honest about what you want and where you are. Set your expectations accordingly.

Double

# CONFESSION

## PANCAKES & PIZZA TOPPINGS

CHARGES:

Premature infatuation, poor flavor judgment, and a consistent inability to read the room.

WEAPONS OF CHOICE:

Midnight carbs, unsolicited commentary, and emotional overreach disguised as charm.

# DOUBLE CONFESSION: PANCAKES & PIZZA TOPPINGS

As I navigated early attempts to discover and implement my dating manifesto, I stumbled across some very interesting men with interesting stories, jobs, and agendas. Some I liked more than they liked me, and some, it was the opposite.

But while dating can be tedious and the desire for love couldn't be more serious, the process of meeting new people can also be fun and lighthearted. Each of us needs to figure out our own rhythm and keep an open mind, while maintaining healthy boundaries and clarity about what we're looking for in the first place.

I was becoming proud of my ability to have fun, not get too attached too early, not compromise, and still enjoy the company of some great guys. I could simply be present and allow them to tell me, and show me, who they are and what they want.

# EXHIBIT A:
## MIDNIGHT PANCAKES

He worked for a local news station. A funny and charming extrovert with a delightful sense of adventure. His conversations were genuine and forthright. He had hobbies and we shared some interests like music and board games.

So, when we were texting late one night and he said,

"I'm hungry. Do you want to go get some pancakes?"

"Now? It's almost midnight! Sure, why not?"

I could hear the summer adventure calling.

"Perfect. I'll come and pick you up in 15 minutes."

I quickly brushed my teeth, got dressed for midnight pancakes, and hopped into the front seat of his car. I was looking forward to our midnight snack! In the ten-minute drive from my house to the restaurant, we see a few cars speed by us along with a couple of police vehicles. He is immediately interested and begins to check his phone for alerts from the station.

"I really should follow this story. You don't mind, do you?"

"I guess not. Can't say I've ever chased a news story with a news man before!"

An hour later, I politely nudge him to remind him about our original mission. I was getting hungry and it was already after 1:00 am. Another thirty minutes pass and he pulls over to get gas. I am grateful for the pit stop. When I emerge from the restrooms, I see him collecting snacks.

"Do you want anything?" he asks.

"Well, if we aren't getting pancakes, I guess I'll grab something."

As I'm making my selection, I see him check out and head back to the car. I paid for my own snacks and made a mental note. I was no longer his date. I had been reduced to just a cute sidekick. Back in the car, I asked him to take me home. I was too tired to unpack what I just experienced.

Our next few encounters were progressively disappointing. It would start out great and then somehow get derailed by work or a call or something that required his full attention, while I waited for a date that would never resume.

Romance was officially depleted.
And still no pancakes.

# EXHIBIT B:
## PIZZA TOPPINGS

He was already seated on the coffee shop patio with a latte in hand when I arrived. He stood to greet me with a hug and immediately said,

"You're bigger than you look in your pictures."

I paused to consider my response. "Wow. Okay," I said. "Nice to meet you too. Do you still want me to sit down?"

He nodded. I wasn't convinced, but sometimes curiosity is stronger than pride. So, I decided to stay.

I sat and listened while he talked about how depressed he was. How he was between jobs. How he was estranged from his son. And still, somehow, managed to circle back to my weight a few more times. I stayed polite. Curious. Until I wasn't. After one too many jabs, I cut him off:

"Listen. Here's how I see it. Appearance is a preference. Everyone has them. Just like pizza toppings. If you don't like mushrooms on your pizza… don't blame the mushroom."

The date didn't last much longer.

As we stood up to part ways, he chivalrously motioned for me to go ahead of him. Then, as I walked past, he reached for my waist and tried to kiss me. He missed my mouth.

After the date, I expected radio silence. Prayed for it, even. But no. The next day, he sent me a Facebook friend request. Turns out? He knew my best friend and their whole family. He asked me on a second date.

I respectfully declined. Thank you, but no. You don't get to insult the toppings and still get the whole slice.

## INSIGHT UNCOVERED

Some dates end with a first kiss. Others just leave you hangry and questioning your life choices.

These encounters sharpened my skills. I got better at spotting the red flags, trusting my gut, and recognizing that "quirky charm" is sometimes just emotionally stunted chaos in a handsome package.

If the vibes are off, there's no need to stay for the coffee or hold out for the pancakes. You won't be everyone's favorite pie, so just go home and make your own damn pizza.

## CASE FILE No. 05

# TERMS OF PARTNERSHIP

## CHARGES:

- UNLIKELY PAIRING
- FAILURE TO QUARANTINE
- UNCLEAR TERMS OF ENDEARMENT

## CASE STATUS:

ROMANCE RETIRED WITH HONORS.

# 05: TERMS OF PARTNERSHIP

### Alias: The Introvert

---

**CHARGES:**

Unlikely Pairing. Failure to Quarantine.
Unclear Terms of Endearment.

**CASE STATUS:**

Romance retired with honors.

---

It was early summer. I had just removed all but that one dating app, clearly not designed to be deleted.

I'd recently ended things with the Painter for the third and last time and completed a six-month workshop on "Embodying Feminine Energy." Because, of course, the problem must be me and my masculine intensity, right? I was trying something new: saying yes to possibilities. I headed to Colorado for a week of remote work with a great view.

While there, I tried again to delete the last remaining dating app. But why not swipe while I'm here? That's when an artsy black and white photo appeared in my feed. A broodingly handsome, clearly artsy guy with kind eyes. He looked like the kind of man who smelled like cedar wood and coffee and could quote Nietzsche or Nina Simone on command. He would've never made it through my old filters. Politically, we were miles apart. Spiritually, complete opposites. But I wasn't dating, remember?

I swiped right anyway. We matched. Wait… we matched!

***Enter: The Introvert***

His opening message was clever. Our conversation turned into phone calls almost immediately. We talked all night. I mean all night. Even after he asked me how I voted in the previous election, I deflected.

"I don't think my vote fully represents who I am as a whole human. Do you?"

Somehow, we kept talking. We started dating. We were enjoying each other's company. Enjoying seeing life from a new perspective. He was a modern man. Emotionally intelligent. Still friends with his ex. Ran a marketing agency with a woman he spoke highly of. Healthy relationship with his parents. Completed his fair share of therapy sessions. No unpaid child support or unfinished degrees. A welcome contrast from my recent dating history.

Our connection felt like a breath of fresh air. He was intellectually stimulating, emotionally safe, and surprisingly playful. We had long conversations about politics without resorting to insults. We made room for each other's contradictions. He let me be bold without flinching, and I let him be soft without judgment. We showed up for each other consistently, learning how to fight fairly and love generously.

One month in, he took me out for lunch just to ask me to be his girlfriend. And after responding with an enthusiastic, "Yes!" I panicked.

The Introvert was a man who was showing up sincerely and checked every box I didn't even know I had. He was kind, competent, consistent. Someone who had the ability to communicate despite our differences. Had I been so conditioned to chaos and charismatic dysfunction through modern dating that normal felt suspicious?

As panic set in, I told myself it was all happening too fast. I was being naïve. This was all too good to be true. Trust in my inner voice was faltering. I was in a full spiral. I needed something to steady me. The wise part of me would have called a bestie, but I didn't want to hear what they had to say. I wanted to face my fears. But how, without exposing myself to heartbreak all over again?

Psycho Self had a great idea: Download the dating app again, she said. Just to look. Just to gauge my interest level and openness. Just to make sure. If I was open to dating other people, I would know I needed to slow things down with the Introvert. If I was really committed, I would be on and off the app before anyone was the wiser. Great idea, right?

No. It was a terrible idea. It was self-sabotage.

I matched with a guy who was everything the Introvert wasn't; and everything I used to think I needed. Spiritually aligned. Politically similar. He quoted scripture, played guitar in church, and said all the right things. On paper, he was a perfect match for me. Especially suited to the version of me that existed before the world cracked open in the divorce. But even as we chatted, I could feel it: the click wasn't there. We would probably get along, maybe even make it work, but I wasn't really interested. Not like that.

And somehow, that calmed me down. It confirmed what my gut already knew: I wasn't running toward something better; I was just scared that good could actually be real. That someone kind, consistent, and wildly different from me might still be the right person to try with. I agreed to go to dinner sometime in the future, knowing I would have time to politely cancel and let him know things had gotten serious with someone else.

I felt a weight lift and was excited to lean all the way into my new relationship. Then the Introvert called. His voice shaky.

"Are you talking to anyone else?"
"Absolutely not! I'm excited to be your girlfriend."
"So, you've deleted all the apps. Haven't been online since we became official?"

Shit. I hated that a completely honest answer would send the wrong message. But I'm a terrible liar, so I fessed up. Told him how silly it was. How embarrassed I was to have even needed to go there for some kind of strange validation.

"Well, at least you were honest."

Wait, what?! Honest? Wait. Where was this all coming from? How would he have even known? Are we that much in sync? Nah. Did my bestie spill the beans? Never. The truth was even stranger. The "perfect match" of a guy? It was his cousin. Catfishing me from Florida! After the Introvert told her so many great things about me, she had her doubts. She encouraged him not to trust me and vowed to prove she was right about me. He thought she just needed time to get on board, never imagining she would take matters into her own hands. But instead, she set a trap and I walked straight into it. Her tactics collided with my insecurities and suddenly, even after defending my character, he wasn't sure he could trust me anymore.

Maybe we were moving too fast.
Maybe I wasn't who he thought I was.
Maybe I wanted the guy in the other profile.

I was mortified. Drove straight over so he could see my face, hopefully hear the sincerity in my voice. This was something worth fighting for, so I did. He was also mortified and apologized to me for his cousin's actions. It was a difficult discussion for both of us, but we made it through. That early honesty became the foundation for everything that followed.

Occasionally, the differences in our personalities clashed, but the ability to communicate always brought us back to a deep appreciation of the other and for the kind of relationship we were building. We weren't in a hurry, but we weren't wasting time either. We moved forward like people who believed they had all the time in the world.

He was always clear about how committed he was to us; how much he loved me and my daughter. I felt the same way. My only reservation was truly wondering if he was ready for a long-term commitment given that he had only had a few months between me and the end of his 17-year common law marriage. He was always quick to reassure me. Our relationship seemed to just keep expanding and growing. We spent the holidays together, met the family. I didn't really connect with his parents, and he admitted he felt a little uncomfortable at my parents' house too.

Looking back, maybe that mattered more than we admitted.

He connected with my daughter in a way I desperately needed at just the right time for her. She loved him and got very attached. But in her early teen years, there were a lot of conflicts that he got caught up in. He would occasionally say things like "This is why I never wanted to be a dad." But quickly follow those up with "I love her though. I just want to help however I can."

We supported each other through difficult work situations. First, his partnership that brought him to town came to an end. Then, my employer decided to sell their business, so I was facing change as well. He suggested we try doing something together.

"Are you serious? That's a terrible idea!" I said.
"What if we break up?"
"We aren't breaking up. We are great together."
"You and I both know that break ups happen. It makes me nervous."
"Listen. We can work through anything. Besides, I cannot imagine a scenario where we aren't married by the end of next year."

That sentence hit me like a warm tidal wave. I was thrilled and terrified all at once. My heart wanted to believe it, to wrap itself in the safety of his certainty. But another part of me—the part that had loved and lost before—couldn't help but flinch. I wanted it to be true. I wanted to believe we were unbreakable.

But the truth was, I'd imagined plenty of scenarios. Some lovely, others devastating. His confidence was beautiful, but it didn't erase my caution. It only made me hope harder that this time would be different. And for a while, I fully enjoyed the luxury of that hope.

We moved forward like a team. Launching the business, splitting responsibilities, dreaming about what we could build together in love and in work. We had a name, a brand, even long-term plans. We talked through contingencies: What if we broke up? Who keeps what? It felt responsible, not cynical. We were grown-ups and found the terms of partnership easy to navigate together.

Then came the visit to see his mother. When he returned home, he looked distant. Guarded. Different. Finally, I asked, "What happened?"

"She asked if I was ready to get married. I am, but it just got me thinking."

He had always reassured me before. Always said "yes" without hesitation. But this time, there was silence. Hesitation. Doubt. I felt the shift in him. I didn't panic. Not right away. I gave him space. I held onto the hope.

Then came the unimaginable scenario: COVID. The world shut down around us.

My three-day trip to visit my daughter turned into three weeks. No one could have imagined the impact it would have on all of us. Businesses failed. Schools stopped. Flights canceled. The ability to plan ahead evaporated. We were faced with choices we had no way to prepare to make. We were all in the same storm, but each person's boat was very different.

I assumed we'd hunker down together. Create a family circle and weather the storm as a unit. But instead, he pulled away. First emotionally. Then physically. Closeness was replaced by video chats.

I believed him when he said he was giving me space to navigate my daughter's education and the risks to my aging parents. But I didn't just want support. I needed a partner. Someone who could meet me on the front lines when life got hard. Who wouldn't retreat into solitude while I stood outside, soaked and shivering, figuring things out alone. If we were going to build a life together, get married, raise a family, and run a business, I had to know he wouldn't fold when things got real. That he wouldn't just cheer me on from a safe distance but help carry the weight when I was out of options.

But instead, he withdrew. Into himself. Into silence. I was left holding everything we were building. Alone. And that loneliness felt louder because I wasn't asking for perfection. I was asking for presence.

The space just kept growing. He grew quieter. He stopped calling as often. The laughter faded. I began to lose him to isolation altogether. Only when he decided to drive to visit a friend in Colorado did I hear something I hadn't heard in his voice in weeks—lightness. Humor even. It broke my heart to realize that same lightness and humor was truly fading from our relationship.

So, when he called to let me know his friend offered to share space if he wanted to relocate to Colorado, even temporarily, I knew immediately in my heart it was what would be best for him. When he came back to Texas, he ended our relationship.

He cried. I cried. A part of me firmly believed this was not what either of us wanted. He told me I didn't deserve to be tied to someone struggling with depression again. He was happy in Colorado. He was happy with me. He just couldn't see a way forward.

I tried to explain that supporting him when he was depressed wasn't the same as my ex. He wasn't mean when he was depressed. The whole world was a mess. We could face this together. I still loved him. He told me he had made promises to himself not to get stuck in Texas forever and he knew it wasn't a good time for me and my daughter to relocate. Plus, the offer from his friend was for him, not us. He had to choose himself.

He said he understood if I wanted to walk away from the business too. I looked him dead in the eye and said:

"I'm not about to lose my relationship and my livelihood all in one day. Try again."

Looking back, it might have been easier to let them both go. But I couldn't imagine a scenario where we would just walk away completely. So, we continued working side by side, building our business, pretending everything was fine while everything had changed. It was excruciating to love someone, see them every day, and not be able to be with them. No flirting. No lingering glances. No asking for emotional support or sharing how I really felt.

What stung the most was that I couldn't even be angry. He hadn't betrayed me. He hadn't lied. He had simply honored his boundaries, and we were both committed to making the business work. That made it harder, not easier. There was no enemy. No villain. Just two people figuring out how to be partners, just not romantic ones.

It was in that quiet ache; I was brought back to a space where love meant wanting what was truly best for the person you love. It wasn't about possession or promises. It was about freedom.

It took a little bit of time, but ultimately, I fully supported his decision to end the relationship. I supported his move to Colorado. Even if it meant letting go of something I still wanted.

Because that's what real love required of me then: not to fight for the version of us I had hoped for, but to honor the version of him that needed space to heal and grow. Before our new rhythm would be possible, there was one more turning point.

In December, I faced a sudden health complication that nearly took my life. Hospitalized during a time when COVID restrictions limited visitors and my family couldn't be there for longer than a few days. Without hesitation, the Introvert stepped up. He took care of my daughter, managed the business, turned off my inbox, and showed up for me in every possible way. Nearly every day for a month, he came by bringing humor, presence, and just enough distraction to keep my spirits intact.

In that fragile space, the physical distance between us faded again. I felt surrounded by his love for me. One afternoon, I finally asked, "Am I the only one struggling with my feelings here?"

He said, softly, "No."

But then added that he was torn between the love we had and the life he envisioned in Colorado.

So, I kissed him, hoping that would be enough to bring him back to me.
Instead, he winced.

I was crushed. Hurt. Offended. That was not the response I was expecting. I thought there would be longing in his eyes. But there was only pain and apology. And in that moment, all my hopes deflated. The sooner he left, the better. I couldn't stay suspended in the in-between. My walls went back up.
I adjusted. I said goodbye. Then, I learned to love him in a whole new way.

As time passed, I could see the misalignments more clearly. The ways we didn't really want the same lifestyle, the differences we had tiptoed around, the goals that quietly diverged.

Love hadn't been a lie. It just wasn't enough.

But love was what fueled our desire for the other to be fully happy within ourselves. Not just for each other.

Months passed. Seasons changed. Slowly, we found our rhythm again. This time as collaborators, not lovers.

Our romantic chapter was over, but the story wasn't.

We still talk almost every day. We still make each other laugh. We still run the business we built together, now with even clearer boundaries and deeper mutual respect. There are no lingering "what ifs," just the quiet confidence of two people who chose not to throw everything away when the shape of their relationship changed.

It's not the ending I imagined, but it's a partnership I'm proud of.

## INSIGHT UNCOVERED

Not every great love ends with a wedding or a forever.

Some end with mutual respect, hard conversations, and the willingness to keep showing up. Just differently than before.

This wasn't a story of betrayal. It was a story of character. Because when others couldn't show up, he did. When the world shut down, when my life was on the line, when I needed care, he came through without hesitation.

We've often said that COVID didn't break us, it just accelerated what time would've revealed eventually. The differences in how we see life, live it, and imagine our future were always there. The pandemic simply forced the conversation early.

This relationship taught me that love isn't always about staying. It's about showing up with integrity, walking away with respect, and being brave enough to preserve the connection even as its form evolves.

Real love holds space for growth. And sometimes, letting go is the most faithful expression of love we have left to give.

# CRIME SPREE

# CRIME SPREE

We did everything right.
At least, that's what the evidence suggested.

We had a healthy breakup. It was mature. Gentle. Thoughtful. There was no villain, no trauma. Just truth. But somehow, that made it worse.

I thought I had done the work. I thought I was ready. I had evidence of my efforts. I had sought input and made improvements. But the universe didn't hand me a final rose. It handed me silence. The breakup handed me something colder than heartbreak: confusion. Because if you can do everything "right" and still end up alone, what's the point? The last time I felt this way was right after the divorce.

So, I paused. I took a whole year off from dating. A full twelve months of quiet. No apps, no meet-cutes, no emotional gymnastics. Just me, my daughter, my healing, my career, and the hum of learning how to be content without the chase. How to be happy being single. No matter how content I felt, I never lost the desire to be in love. Partnered. Married. I would just need to approach things a little differently. So, I pivoted. From romantic idealist to pragmatic dater. From "I hope this is it" to "let's see what happens."

No detours. No delays. Just "Thank you, next."

I started dating in cohorts. If I was going to win this game, I had to play the odds. I hopped online, swiped right until I was out of likes, and sent messages to no more than twenty men at a time. Within a week, a dozen would disappear with no replies, no follow-through. The ones who stayed made up "the cohort." We'd chat for a couple of weeks, then narrow the slate to four or five first dates.

From there? Maybe a few might earn a second round. Once I was down to two, I'd follow my heart and the evidence. It wasn't scientific, but it was structured, and compared to what I'd done before? It felt like progress.

Lots of chats. Lots of dates. Lots of laughs and adventures.

I approached it with clarity and efficiency. If there were red flags, I moved on. If they ended it, I accepted their decision. Quickly. No dragging it out. No over-analysis. No wallowing for weeks. No chasing closure. The sooner I moved forward, the sooner I could find the right match. I was filled with hope and humor about what lay ahead, and I didn't look back. This was about possibility, not about promiscuity; about reclaiming joy, flirtation, and maybe even a little bit of confidence.

It wasn't until much later, when the dust settled, that I could see how far I'd gone off course from my true desire to find a healthy, lasting relationship. When I could see what I'd done to myself.

Every investigator hits a wall. This was mine. Staring at the stack of case files with over twenty crime scenes in less than a year, it was clear that somewhere along the line, I had stopped looking for "the one" and started chasing chemistry. I had gone rogue – ignoring protocol, refusing backup, and justifying my actions to the brass.

If the full case files were about the relationships I tried to build, these were the ones I tried to bury. The ones that were met with more objectivity than optimism. The ones where it stopped being about compatibility and devolved into chemistry, craving, boredom, or the simple need to feel something… fast. Where I wanted to be wanted so badly, I skipped the background check. I wouldn't call them all mistakes. I wouldn't call them wise, either.

Be warned, some of these crime scenes deserve trigger warnings. As the dating casualties piled up, my ability to walk away unscathed became more difficult. I am not including these stories to shock you. I'm writing them because they happened and because they shaped how I saw myself, how I would show up, and shut down, in every case file that followed

***Welcome to the Crime Spree.***

## THE MARRYING KIND

**CHARGE:** Rush to commitment and 2nd degree sincerity
**WEAPON OF CHOICE:** Heartfelt declarations at sunset

He was handsome. Grounded. Thoughtful. A real estate developer and wood importer. Raised in Canada, shaped by Singapore, now living in Dallas, and somehow still ready to relocate for love.

We met online. His messages were articulate and kind, his faith strong but never performative. There were no games. No chasing. Just intentionality wrapped in a warm accent and an eagerness I hadn't felt from anyone in a long time.

He drove in for our first date. I planned a full day of connection. A long walk-through nature. A quiet museum. Tapas and conversation. A late dinner and drinks under soft lights and warmer stars.

It felt... safe. Almost cinematic. An amazing start.

Over dessert, I was bracing for a second date invite. He was ready to define the future of our relationship. I was just getting started. I let him know I wanted to take things a little slower. Keep getting to know each other.

Was it honesty that led me to share my cohort approach or self-protection dressed in transparency? Was I being picky or just honest? Either way, he was unimpressed. We said our goodbyes at the end of the night. And never spoke again.

**INSIGHT UNCOVERED:**

Sometimes the story checks every box but still doesn't open your heart. Nice doesn't always mean right, and not every man ready for marriage is the man you're meant to choose.

# THE SWINGER

**CHARGE:** Grand Ghosting in the First Degree
**WEAPON OF CHOICE:** An untraceable exit strategy

He came in like a dating app unicorn: charming, clever, and claiming to want something real. We both had only children. We both knew how to be alone. We both respected each other's demanding work schedules.

He was two hours away and made the trip to see me often. Always with a hotel room. Always with great breakfast. He spoke to me in a deliberate, intimate, disarming way. In a way that made me feel seen. Desired. Respected. He also taught me a lot. About how he decided to embrace ENM (ethical non-monogamy). About sex in general and things I didn't even know about my own sexuality.

We played Wordle in bed. We shared stories about past relationships, our heartbreaks and failures, and described the future like we were building something newer, better, more intentional. The first time I made the trip to visit him, he had a personalized gift basket waiting for me on the counter. A whole gift basket with my name engraved on the gifts. I didn't even mind that he had his assistant put it together. I didn't care that he had most certainly done this before.

It was steamy, playful, and wildly affirming. It didn't take long for me to get attached. A couple months in, I invited him to accompany me to a black-tie charity gala. I wanted to dress up, he owned a tuxedo, and this was a guy who clearly knew how to work a room. Not just the bedroom. Plus, I wanted to introduce him to my friends. He said he was ready. A week before the event, I double-checked that work wouldn't get in the way:

"Are we still good for next weekend?"
"Absolutely. I'm looking forward to it."
The day before the gala, I send an excited, "See you tonight!"
Then get his reply, "I'm sorry. I can't do this anymore."
I called multiple times, but no answer. I texted a couple more times, but no reply.

Just like that… poof! No explanation. Just digital dust.

**INSIGHT UNCOVERED:**

Not everyone follows through on their promises nor lives up to their own hype. While I may have hoped for a more respectful ending, I learned the truth of his lack of reciprocity early and didn't internalize the disappearing act. The Dating Manifesto kept me and Psycho Self grounded. That's progress.

# TINDER TIME WARP

**CHARGE:** Unlawful time travel and emotional trespassing
**WEAPON OF CHOICE:** Crippling self-doubt

I was out of town for work. Back in my home state of New Mexico, with a couple nights to burn. Out of curiosity (and maybe a little boredom), I opened Tinder.

That's when I saw him: a guy from high school I had a hopeless crush on in Spanish class. He was a senior. I was a freshman. He dated my friend and never knew how I felt.

We'd kept in touch on Facebook over the years, so I swiped right. More for the cosmic coincidence than anything romantic. We matched.

It didn't take long before we were comparing schedules to figure out when and where we could connect and catch up. Conveniently, he would be driving through town a few days later. Since he was an old friend, I broke my own rule and invited him over to my house.

What followed was a full afternoon of heartfelt reconnection. Two decades of memories unpacked in a living room that wasn't meant for casual daters. We laughed. We reflected. We looked back through the lens of who we thought we were and saw how deeply skewed our perspectives had been.

He was shocked I ever had a crush on him and said I hadn't aged a day. I was shocked to learn about the ocean of self-doubt he still carried from decades earlier, and from his somewhat recent divorce.

The conversation turned into canoodling, as these things do. Then I caught the look on his face. It was the same look as the one I'd seen before in men like The Painter. He didn't just want connection; he wanted a time machine. To see himself in the way I saw him all those years ago.

My memory of him from high school felt safer than the man he'd become. He needed admiration more than affection, and a physical reminder of the man he never quite believed himself to be.

We gave each other what we could. Nostalgia, pity, and the kind of closeness that was more about memory than magnetism.

**INSIGHT UNCOVERED:**

Some people are better left in the form of a childhood crush. Not because they're dangerous but because they collapse under the weight of being remembered as someone they lost along the way. And I've carried enough broken boys to know I'm not here to put anyone back together. That's an inside job.

# SELF-SERVICE ANIMAL

**CHARGE:** Impersonating a Satisfying Lover
**WEAPON OF CHOICE:** Grandiose poker tales

This one started with a last-minute date cancellation after weeks of buildup and careful planning. I was out of town, alone in my hotel, and bored. So, I got on the apps and matched with the first decent-looking guy who didn't have existing plans that evening.

We talked for, maybe, 20 minutes before I invited him over to join me in the rooftop pool. Am I really doing this? Yes. In the wake of my agitation toward my original date, I lowered the bar and still managed to trip over it.

Another 20 minutes go by and he showed up with his dog—an unruly "service animal in training" that was more emotional support liability than canine hero. The dog was cute. The man? Less so.

This guy was confident. Arrogant, even. Talked about professional poker. High-stakes games. Massive wins. Tragic losses. Claimed he was worth millions. You know… all the stuff men who bring dogs to hotel hookups usually say.

Thanks to the dog, we skipped the pool and went straight to the bedroom. He was, hands down, the most selfish lover I've ever encountered. No finesse. No curiosity. Just a lot of self-congratulating and bad angles. The dog kept jumping on the bed. I kept mentally exiting the situation.

The next morning, we took the dog for a walk while sipping hotel coffee. He told more stories. Each one bigger than the last. I nodded. I smiled. I walked away with a decent caffeine buzz and the knowledge that I had absolutely gambled and lost.

**INSIGHT UNCOVERED:**

Sometimes, lowering the bar is worse than being stood up. And if the dog has worse training than the man, leave them both at the door.

## SPICY CHAI

**CHARGE:** Repeated acts of seduction with no reciprocation
**WEAPON OF CHOICE:** Undelivered promises

We met in a city so big most dates feel like job interviews with traffic. He was only five minutes away. That never happens.

Tall, dark, and devastating in all the right ways, he met me for drinks and appetizers, and within twenty minutes I had invited him to my side of the booth.

He wasn't my usual type and that was the point. I was intentionally pushing my boundaries, exploring what else might be out there, who else I might connect with when I wasn't trying to repeat my past. And this man?

He was an education. Effortless charm, rich laughter, skin like velvet and voice like heat.

We ended the night in his car, doing things that would later require professional detailing. And for a few months, we spiraled into a perfect cocktail of sensuality, distance, and broken promises.

Every time I visited his city, he made time for me. Expensive drinks. Deep kisses. Amazing sex. He wanted to make me his "baba," take me to his home country, then travel the world together. Buy me jewelry. Take care of me. It was all brilliantly seductive, but something rang hollow in it for me.

The reality was that we only ever saw each other when I came to him. I never received any gifts. He never followed through on visiting my town, and I'm supposed to trust in his grandiose promises? How about we just start with the simple things. No need to lie or exaggerate. And please, please, please, do not make promises you don't intend to keep.

Behind closed doors, Spicy Chai was a force of nature, like something that walked out of the pages of a romance novel. I was confident enough by now to assert some things I'd like to experience with him, and he was always quick to promise the world. The reality was, while I enjoyed every minute, it was more about him than me, and I started to notice a pattern. He avoided reciprocating with me every time. Finally, one night in a hotel, after an amazing dinner out with friends, I pushed the issue. He could get what he wanted right after he fulfilled one of those sexy promises he had made me. He pouted, negotiated, and tried to distract me. When I explained how it only makes sense that we both be able to make requests of each other, he admitted he would never be on the giving end of this topic and didn't understand why I had to make an issue out of it. I knew it was over then and there.

He texted me a month later crying "Baba, I miss you." Then again after a couple of months—on Valentine's Day. I never responded.

**INSIGHT UNCOVERED:**

**A man who's obsessed with getting his needs met but never shows up for yours isn't a partner. He's nothing more than a latte of loneliness. And eventually, you stop drinking.**

## THE FIGHTER

**CHARGE:** Aggravated intensity with premature possession
**WEAPON OF CHOICE:** Competitive affection

He was different. An East Coast guy with a military background and an impressive trophy case. He was a fighter. A trainer. A father.

And unlike Spicy Chai, he seemed to be playing for more than just fun.

Our conversations were intense and deep. We swapped stories, dreams, traumas.

He had a decorated career and big plans for the future. He just needed to clear up some lingering divorce drama and family fallout.

Still, I was cautiously optimistic. I'd been clear about my pace and my boundaries. I let him know I was intentionally getting to know multiple people at the same time to allow things to grow over time. And the Fighter? He seemed confident he could win me over. Invigorated by the competitive challenge.

Our first date was a marathon: brunch, ATV ride through the canyon, and ice cream in the park. Then an impromptu invitation for evening cocktails in his hot tub.

He'd been very clear early on in our conversations: we would not be having sex. He didn't do hookups. I respected that. Appreciated it, even. In the hot tub, it was him who succumbed to the chemistry while giving me a massage. He didn't want to say goodnight just yet. I affirmed my shared attraction but also reminded him of our agreed boundary. I didn't want to be the reason he felt bad in the morning.

That night, he tested his own boundaries, even crossing a line or two he didn't plan on. We were both intoxicated by the hours of time we had spent together. It was well past midnight when I finally started lacing up my shoes to head home. In my tired state, I blurted out that he was a winner in my book and that I'd be having some hard conversations when I got home so I could focus more fully on him.

The mood shifted instantly. His energy turned cold.

He was insulted that I'd spent all day with him while "still talking to other people." I reminded him this was our first in-person date, that I had been upfront about talking with other people online. He insisted to me that I had lied and was clearly disloyal and dishonest. Just like his ex. Just like all women. Not to be trusted.

He held it together long enough to walk me out and confirm lunch plans for the next day. Maybe we both just needed some sleep. The man who showed up to the restaurant was a stranger. Cold. Condescending. Accusatory. He called my morality into question and labeled me incapable of honesty and loyalty. He insisted he wasn't ready for a relationship then punished me for not reading between the lines. He claimed I had seduced him into betraying his own boundaries. This was my fault. I was dumbfounded.

His version of events was a rewrite I didn't recognize. His words were worthy of blood sport and yet, somehow, I didn't take any of it to heart. I just sat there watching him throw punches in my direction.

His reaction wasn't about me. It was about him. I was happy to leave him with his version of things and walk away. When we said goodbye, there was no kiss. Just a hug that could've turned me to ice. He said he needed space to reconsider.

A week later, he resurfaced. Not with softness, but with even more certainty that I was untrustworthy. He did say he appreciated how I empathized with his family and legal woes, and that he might like to call me occasionally for support.

I suggested a therapist.

**INSIGHT UNCOVERED:**

Fast chemistry and depth isn't the same as emotional safety. Some men don't date.
They shadowbox. And when he broke his own boundaries, he needed someone else to absorb the blow.

If a man makes you the villain in his own boundary breach, he was never fighting for love—just fighting himself.

I don't need to spar for affection. And I don't need to prove my character to someone who enters the ring already convinced I'm the opponent.

## THE AUTHOR

**CHARGE:** Involuntary boredom in the first degree
**WEAPON OF CHOICE:** Earnest Monotony

We met on an app. His kids lived in my town, so he had reason to visit often. As an established, published author, his flexible schedule made it easy to see me.

I was intrigued by his maturity, his calm cadence, and the fact that he was a few years ahead in the parenting department. He exuded stability. A slow, intentional pace. Even his traditional approach to dating felt refreshing.

We met for coffee and followed it up with a museum. Classic.

From the moment we met, I wasn't overwhelmed by sexual attraction, but I was intrigued by his intellect and charmed by his creativity.

As we wandered through exhibits, he took his time, discussed meaning and nuance like we were annotating our own first chapter. If it were a movie, that would've been the moment for a slow handhold. A spark. Cue a shared milkshake with two straws and soft jukebox music in the background.

Instead, I got… awkward museum silence and strange physical distance.

By the time we lingered in the parking lot, still talking, I was negotiating with myself. Hoping something would shift. That sparks would flicker.

But then I caught our body language. My arms crossed, his gaze drifting. I was slowly stepping back. He wasn't really looking at me. And I knew.

My body had already decided. I wasn't interested.

We exchanged polite goodbyes and said we should do it again. He never followed up. I never reached out.

Not all stories need a sequel.

**INSIGHT UNCOVERED:**

Sometimes it takes a quiet, harmless date to remind you that curiosity and compatibility aren't the same thing.

He didn't do anything wrong, but my body wouldn't let me pretend it felt right.

## THE EMMY WINNER

**CHARGE:** Distributing fantasy with intent to abandon
**WEAPON OF CHOICE:** Hall-of-fame charisma

He worked for ESPN—had won an Emmy for his work—and was in town for the college football game. He was searching for a local tour guide and someone to wine and dine.

He was sexy as hell. Just my type. That perfect blend of cocky and confident, fun and serious, young and grown. A man's man through and through. It was clear he knew exactly what he was doing.

I recommended a local hot spot, and he was ready to show me a great time. As we took our first sips, I got my bestie's text that her date had gone up in flames. She need her bestie, and a drink. He didn't flinch. Instead, he invited her to join us.

She arrived a few minutes later to a drink waiting for her and open arms from both of us. It didn't take long for him to sweep her off her feet too. Somehow, he held the attention of both of us while making it unmistakably clear who held his interest. A gentle caress to my lower back. A brush of the thigh. A close whisper in my ear when the bar got too loud. I was a goner.

We said goodnight to my friend and kept the night going. Ducked in for foot massages then found another spot for whiskey and cigars. He showed me his favorite travel photos. Told fascinating stories. Described possible meetups in other cities so he wouldn't have to "keep meeting new people." A well-pitched fantasy that I bought hook line and sinker.

That night meandered until we landed in his suite. Let's just say the late-night wrestle match with this former pro athlete deserved a highlight reel of its own. He asked me to stay for breakfast. Lounge in his hotel robe. Room service, great soundtrack, glowing compliments. I lingered. Swooned.

Then came the morning-after mood swing. Somewhere between the eggs and the check, he decided we should talk politics and religion. More combatively than curiously. Like he was looking for a debate to end a honeymoon. I suggested we find lighter subjects. He refused. The glamour was wearing off.

Still, at the door, he kissed me like a man who meant it.

Told me not to go far. He wanted to see me again before he left town. I cleared my schedule. His text never came.

**INSIGHT UNCOVERED:**

When someone knows exactly how to make you feel chosen, it's easy to forget they've done it before. Many times.

I sometimes wonder how many cities are in his highlight reel and whether I made the top plays. I was far from the first woman in his lineup, and I would definitely not be the last. But damn, did he put on a good show.

## THE DIPLOMAT

**CHARGE:** Sexual violation
**WEAPON OF CHOICE:** Diplomatic charm and cuisine

Finally, a nice dinner with a chivalrous man. He was well-spoken, successful, intentional and rooted in faith. He was a dignitary back in his home country. Accustomed to status, admiration, and getting what he wanted.

We enjoyed interesting conversation, a great meal, and shared values despite coming from different cultures. He had a presence that exuded leadership and made it easy to let my walls down. Since I was leaving town the next day, he leapt at the opportunity to reconnect over lunch the next day.

We decided to meet at his place and go from there. As I pulled into the parking lot, something in me stirred. An unfamiliar discomfort I couldn't yet name. Something told me to share my location with a friend, just in case, even though I'd never done that before.

Then, I sent a quick text that I had arrived. But instead of him joining me outside, he invited me up to meet his roommate and try a bit of his home cooked traditional cuisine. I was thrown off by the change in plans and expressed my desire to still go out for lunch. He assured me we would. Soon. Then suggested we give his roommate the living room while we went to his bedroom for more privacy. When I asked why we couldn't stay in the living room, he chuckled and said that was the only TV in the apartment. I even suggested that I continue talking with his roommate while he got ready to leave.

He insisted, politely.

In the bedroom, there was nowhere to sit but the bed. I expressed my discomfort to him. Something told me not to sit down. That we should leave for lunch. But I brushed off those feelings and decided to trust the man who took me to dinner the night before. It was just conversation.

It didn't take long for everything to shift. I didn't mind the kiss, but made it clear I didn't want to go any further. What followed wasn't violent. But it wasn't right. It wasn't consent.

I instantly froze. He treated that as permission. I resisted. I kept saying no. My legs clenched shut like a bear trap. He kept trying to convince me it was what I wanted. Diplomatically, of course. I couldn't mentally access a way to stop him without making things worse. So, I complied to a point. Minimized the physical impact.

I laid still. Stunned silence filled the room as I politely excused myself to the bathroom to clean up. Once I was safe behind a locked door, I kept repeating one instruction to myself: Get out. Still disoriented, I nodded when he offered to walk me to my car. Such a gentleman.

I didn't cry. I didn't scream. I didn't call the police. Everything in me locked down and pushed forward.

As I drove away, my mind replayed the scene like surveillance footage. The color of the walls, where he kept the extra toilet paper, the direction of my car in the parking lot. I kept telling myself how much worse it could have been. How lucky I was. Like someone who walked away from a car crash with only minor injuries.

This wasn't the first time I'd found myself in a moment that crossed a line, but it was the first time I couldn't talk myself into believing it was just awkward or a misunderstanding. This wasn't nothing, but there was no version of this story that ended with justice. Only the quiet understanding that something had been taken and that there was nothing to be done with that knowledge but carry it.

I told myself I had to keep moving. So, I minimized it. I told a trusted friend on my drive home, then acted like it was just another date that didn't go anywhere.

But underneath the composure, something cracked. I started to wonder when, exactly, my search for love had turned into something else. When resilience had slipped into risk. When proving I was desirable started costing me my sense of safety.

I let the fear move through me on the long drive home. Then I buried it.

He texted me later that night to make sure I got home safely and was confused about why I didn't want to see him again. I didn't explain further. I had been diplomatic enough.

## INSIGHT UNCOVERED:

This wasn't heartbreak. It was harm.

What stayed with me wasn't just what he did, it was what happened inside me afterward. How quickly I assessed the damage. How efficiently I moved forward. How instinct took over and carried me out.

Freezing protected me in the moment. Moving on protected me afterward. Both were survival, not weakness. But what lingered wasn't fear, it was clarity.

I didn't lose trust in myself that day. I was reminded to trust the small signals I had learned to override. The quiet unease. The internal pause. The moment something feels off and politeness tries to take the wheel.

I saw how often I had prioritized being agreeable over

being safe. How easily I had been trained to manage other people's comfort instead of my own protection. How I had acted as if I owed men softness, patience, or explanation even when everything in me wanted to leave.

They would tell their own version of the story or forget me altogether. Either way, I owed them nothing. Because, if a man doesn't respect your no, he never respected your yes.

# ESCAPE ROOM ARTIST

**CHARGE:** Capacity misalignment.
**WEAPON OF CHOICE:** Good intentions without bandwidth

We dated for three months. He worked for an airline, which made it easy for him to jet over to see me, and I was more than happy to return the favor. He wanted a relationship. I was ready to be out of the revolving door of interludes and intermittent affection.

We watched movies, tackled puzzles, escaped rooms, and dove into long, winding conversations. He was intelligent, a veteran, and fully transparent about his years of therapy and ongoing mental health efforts.

I never felt like I had to perform for him. I could be my own nerdy self and enjoy simple dates. It was... Easy. Honest. Fun. And because it was, I didn't notice when ease quietly turned into expectation.

But the deeper we got into the relationship, the more I started to notice how his mental health operated. As present as he could be, his diagnosis served as a barrier between us. Thick protection that kept him from ever having to decenter himself. I wasn't competing with another woman. I was competing with his coping mechanisms, and they had seniority.

His struggles were real, and they kept reminding me not to expect too much from someone who was 'already doing his best.'

A couple months in, I visited his city and stayed at his place for the first time. That's when the curtain lifted. Nothing dramatic happened. It was just a little too soon to be that far inside someone's world.

Or maybe it wasn't. Because by this point in my journey, I'd started treating conflict as data. How someone responds to pressure, discomfort, or disagreement says more about their history than it does about me.

I recognized some familiar patterns: subtle victimhood, unacknowledged entitlement, the way empathy became currency. We continued to patch things together the best we could and talk intelligently through conflicts.

I changed focus to my upcoming birthday weekend. We decided to take a trip to celebrate. It was fun to play tourist. Share good meals. But that was the weekend when all the little things added up.

In a moment where I tried to show up with vulnerability, I was met with indifference while he watched a game show.

I sat there, naked in bed on my birthday, and he didn't so much as glance in my direction until after the Wheel of Fortune credits rolled. That's when I knew. I am not satisfied here. I am not going to settle for a life of after-thought birthday sex with my partner. I am allowed to want more.

I'll confess. I took the easy way out. I called to let him know I had been thinking things over and ultimately, I was not going to be able to give him what he needed. He had complained at one point about my busyness and divided attention, so I leaned on that for my exit strategy.

Nobody deserves to feel less than just because I decided to go find something different.

## INSIGHT UNCOVERED:

The lessons I learned were heavier than my relationship with the Escape Room Artist.

He was trying. We both were. I believe that. But trying isn't the same as having the capacity to meet your partner's needs. Therapy gave him language. Medication gave him stability. Neither guaranteed emotional availability.

For years, I carried a quiet belief that my marriage might have survived if only mental health support had entered the picture. This relationship dismantled that theory. I learned that support helps but doesn't replace intentional growth.

Insight doesn't automatically unlock behavior.

Relationships aren't escape rooms. Staying longer doesn't mean you're any closer to winning. Sometimes the bravest move is walking out.

He wasn't a villain. He wasn't withholding. He was operating at the edge of what he could offer. I had to face my part too. I enjoyed the ease but couldn't show up for him the way that mattered most to him. I appreciated his efforts, but I couldn't keep shrinking my expectations to protect his comfort.

Capacity misalignment isn't cruelty. It's reality. And ours didn't match.

# THE SADIST

**CHARGE:** Concealed kinks and assault
**WEAPON OF CHOICE:** Unpacked boxes

We met in broad daylight. Shared a sandwich in the park. It was easy. Light.

He worked in finance. Clean cut. Polite. Charming. Stable. The kind of guy your therapist recommends after a few too many late-night mistakes.

I was happy to accept his invitation to dinner the next night at his new place. He was in the middle of moving in and said he just needed a good reason to get out the cookware. He lived alone, just him and his dogs.

Over dinner, I noticed two medium-sized boxes labeled "Toys."

I asked about them, flirtatiously.
He smiled, said they belonged in the bedroom, and changed the subject.

We ate. Talked about work, dogs, family. Then moved to the couch and eventually, the bedroom.

That's where he changed. Like a switch flipped. The warmth disappeared. Consent became assumed.

At first, I tried to keep it light. Playful. Then firmer. Direct.

He didn't hear me. Or chose not to.
He said he was holding back. Going easy on me.
That I was lucky he hadn't unpacked those boxes yet.
Like that was supposed to reassure me.

My breath went shallow. I wasn't negotiating anymore. I just wanted out.

My body shifted into survival mode while my mind went razor-sharp. I don't remember exactly what I said, only that when the moment came. I took it. I got out.

Safe at home, I sat alone in the dark. Everything hurt. When I finally decided to shower, I saw his handiwork in the mirror. Bruises. Bite marks. All in places clothes could hide.

I stared long enough to stop bargaining with myself. Long enough to admit what this was. I took pictures. For me. To remember where I had been and where I would never go again. Proof of how dark things had gotten. How far I had fallen.

A few days later, at a concert with my best friend, she asked how dinner went. I didn't answer. I just looked at her and shifted my blouse.

She gasped. Pulled me into a hug. "Are you ok?"

"Of course not. But It's over. In a few weeks, it'll be like it never happened."

She urged me to slow down. To take a break. Wise counsel from a loving friend.

I assured her I wasn't ignoring what happened. I was facing it. I'd survived something real. It was going to take time to trust again, but I refused to lose the trust I'd built with myself.

I'd come too far. This wasn't a misunderstanding. It wasn't chemistry gone wrong or desire misread. This was the violent handiwork of a sadist that marked the end of something.

I didn't leave that experience with clarity. All I knew was that I couldn't keep pretending this was all just bad luck.

**INSIGHT UNCOVERED:**

Sometimes the most dangerous men are the ones who seem safe—measured, polite, and controlled—until privacy removes the need for restraint.

His hands weren't the weapon.
His indifference to my humanity was.

Sometimes the most dangerous patterns aren't the ones we encounter. They're the ones we don't yet know how to stop.

## AUTOPSY REPORT

What I carried out of that night wasn't just bruises. It was the realization that this spree was no longer accidental. It was dangerous and costly. It was no longer moving me forward. It was wearing me down.

I was no longer hunting hearts. I was chasing heat. These weren't love stories. They were flash fires. Some seductive. Some scarring. Most built on broken compasses. I kept saying I was "just having fun," but the truth? I was testing a theory.

After my husband looked me in the eye and said he'd never been sexually attracted to me, and doubted anyone else ever would, I had to know for myself: Was that true? Would anyone see me as desirable again? Could I see myself that way?

So, I put the theory on trial.

And I learned fast: sex is the easy part. It doesn't matter how old, short, or fat you are. Sex can be transactional whether money is exchanged or not. Bodies can just be treated like bodies.

But connection? Care? Chemistry that lingers after the clothes come off? That requires more vulnerability. More capacity.

What I found surprised me: I could feel sexy. Beautiful. Wanted. Even powerful. I learned what I like, what I don't. I learned that every experience is only as electric as the connection behind it. I discovered that a single, passionate kiss can tell you everything you need to know about physical chemistry. No further investigation required.

Yes, I still get tempted to swipe right. But something's shifted. Now the echoes after an empty thrill rings louder than the thrill itself. The spree didn't end with a bang. It ended with a whisper from deep inside that said:

This isn't who we are anymore.
This isn't helping anymore.

Because honestly? I've come to respect myself, and men, more than I ever did during the hook-up era. That doesn't mean I walked away healed. No, I walked away hurting and hungry. Numb in some places. Addicted in others.

Out of the spree, but not yet fully free.

Because what the spree really gave me was a bad habit. Escapism disguised as adventure. Validation masquerading as chemistry. Loneliness, dressed up in the fantasy of forever.

I stopped swiping for a moment, but the part of me still searching? She wasn't quite finished.

# THE INVESTIGATION CONTINUES

# THE INVESTIGATION CONTINUES

## No Longer a Rookie

---

The early cases taught me to look closer. To examine not just who I was dating, but what I was hoping to find in them. What was still healing in me.

I had mistaken admiration for intimacy. Confused effort with alignment. Tried to redeem people who didn't ask for help, only access to my body or my heart.

By now, I'd gotten blood on my hands. Broken hearts, including my own. This wasn't a string of accidents. This was a pattern. I had been at this long enough. I was no longer a rookie.

Every encounter left a clue. The prevailing truth was this: I am the common thread. The one constant across every confession.

I wasn't just collecting evidence anymore. I was building a profile of myself. Deciphering who I was, what I needed, what I could handle, and what I refused to tolerate again.

But there was one truth I hadn't admitted yet.<br>
Not out loud.<br>
Not even to myself.

Until now, I had always entered new encounters with hope, optimism, curiosity, a flicker of belief that this time might be different. But after the heartbreak of the Introvert and the wreckage left by the Sadist, I didn't swipe with hope in my heart.

I swiped with muscle memory.

With just enough detachment to make it through the small talk.
With just enough charm to keep the spotlight off the bruises.

I wasn't looking for love anymore. I was looking for proof. That I could still feel something. That I could still choose someone. That maybe a functional connection was still possible, even if my heart had gone dark. Even if I wasn't offering the parts of myself I used to.

And that's when I realized the thing I never thought I'd be:
I was now emotionally unavailable.

The roles had reversed. I was no longer chasing. No longer dreaming. I had no appetite for romanticizing the future.

I was just trying not to disappear completely. And where I might have once paused to reflect, to recalibrate, to sit still long enough to heal—instead I suppressed the heartache and the violence and went looking for my next escape.

I told myself I was fine. I was the furthest thing from fine.
I was worn out. Walled up. Shut down.
But pain is a strong numbing agent and habit a convincing driver.

Numb and callous, I started swiping out of habit. Not to find someone to love, but to put distance between me and the recent crime scenes. Any new case file felt safer than sitting too long with the last one.

CASE FILE No. 06

# THE ARRANGEMENT

HOTEL

CHARGES:

- EMOTIONAL MANIPULATION
- PUSHING BOUNDARIES
- SELF-DECEPTION

CASE STATUS:

CLOSED. NO RETRIAL NECESSARY.

# 06: THE ARRANGEMENT

### Alias: The Married Man

---

**CHARGES:**

Emotional Manipulation, Pushing Boundaries, Self-deception

**CASE STATUS:**

Closed. No Retrial Necessary.

---

I wasn't looking for love. Just something to take my mind of the Sadist. Something low stakes but satisfying. A fling without feelings, a distraction to file under "fun while it lasted."

So, I went shopping. Not for a boyfriend—god, no—but for a delicious little escape. I was done playing the nice girl who waits around for emotionally constipated men to figure out what they want and done acting like hookups were going to magically blossom into something more.

Whole books and blogs have been written about dating apps, contemplating whether they're the best or worst thing to happen to relationships. I resonate with both sides. They can be soul-sucking wastelands of shirtless mirror selfies and cryptic one-word bios, or they can be fast, convenient, and perfectly transactional.

That day, I wasn't scrolling for compatibility. I was skimming for chemistry. If you're emotionally unavailable and you know it, clap your hands!

Welcome to the largest farmers market of barely contained thirst on the planet.

His profile may as well have been lined in flashing neon lights:

- ***"I travel constantly for work."*** Perfect. He won't be around long enough to disrupt my life.
- ***"Real women have curves."*** Check. This body is total hourglass.
- ***"A fantastic smile gets me every time."*** Cue the inner minx. He has no idea.
- ***"I have a very playful Dom streak - not crazy or demeaning."*** Wait... What?
- ***"My location - 1.2 miles away"*** Stop. Hold my drink.

***Enter: The Married Man***

My curiosity wasn't just piqued. It was practically vibrating. Playful. In control. Preferably discreet. It felt like ordering validation and escape à la carte.

I knew I matched his physical type, and he did mine. More dad bod than gym bro. Add in intelligent quick wit, a velvety smooth voice, and a devilish grin and I'm toast.

Swipe Right. Instant Match.

I message first. Within seconds, the chat bubble is active and he responds.

Damn. He is witty.

He is also leaving town in a few short hours. I could have just wished him a safe journey. But instead, I ask,

"Wanna grab a quick drink before you hit the road?"

I haven't even met him yet, and I can feel the smirk in his response.

"I don't think drinking before a l long road trip is a great idea but meeting you sure is. How about a nice, iced tea? You pick the place. It's your town."

A little logistical banter and we had our destination … and 90 minutes.

The vibe was playful. Banter via text and in person was seamless. He was wearing his corporate uniform and knew how to play the gentleman. I suggest an appetizer and he says he's not hungry, but I should get to have whatever I want.

Ok, Casanova. Captain cocky with the non-stop innuendos and double entendres.

And somehow, I found myself entertained. We sat there for over an hour without a beat in conversation. Mainly because he was talking about himself, his military experience, his professional accomplishments. His seedy conquests and red-light district escapades overseas.

As I sat, smiling, enjoying my iced tea and queso, tossing in the occasional slow draw from my straw or curling my hair around my finger as he waxed on. I got the memo, loud and clear, that he was a charming and intelligent cad. And I had nailed the role of the curvy, mysterious stranger that could somehow keep up with him.

"So, what's your play? A girl in every town?"

"In every town? My job takes me to 5 different states!"

"And the wife is none the wiser, I suppose."

Silence. I'm convinced that the background music even stopped. His head tilts to the side, eyes narrow, somewhat suspicious and somewhat bewildered. My eyebrows raise and eyes widen, realizing my question asked in jest was more of a straight arrow.

I say nothing. Just wait and grin. This should be good.

"We have an understanding. An arrangement. What happens on the road, stays on the road."

"Is she aware of this understanding?"

This is where a less experienced hustler would have bristled, but he was intrigued. Attracted. He had met a match worthy of his charms. His expression led me to imagine him thinking, *"If I play my cards right, this could be fun. Real fun."*

Game on.

"Very aware. It's been going on for years. My whole career. She stays at home with our kids and doesn't have to work. I don't do anything to make waves."

You see, I'm no home wrecker. And I'm not going to endorse keeping secrets or lying to your partner. Besides, he's leaving town in 20 minutes. I needed to go meet my friends for a concert. I saw no harm in flirting. I was still trying to put the Sadist behind me, and this was helping.

"Guess I should wish you safe travels home. Thanks for meeting me. I had fun."

"I'm glad we did this. But I just found out I don't have to leave until tomorrow. I got a text from a customer while we were talking. If you want to continue this, I'm staying at a great hotel just down the road, Room 177. I'd love to see you again before I leave town."

"Walk me out."

And like the gentleman he was, he paid the tab, offered his hand as I stood, held the door and walked beside me. Just close enough to gently guide me by the small of my back as we neared my car door. He waited as I turned around, and before I could lean in for the goodbye hug, he pulled me in for a kiss.

Damn. He is smooth.

It was a perfect flirtatious encounter. No need to extend this into the pointless frivolity it promised. But I could feel the gnawing of curiosity throughout the evening. The sensation of that kiss stayed on replay in my head for hours as I considered his invitation.

Should I go? This is a terrible idea.
Would I go? Of course I would.
And there would be a cost. I just hadn't calculated it yet.

I convinced myself I would just enjoy one more drink with him. Maybe one more kiss. Bruises from the sadist were still visible, and I didn't care to reveal those to anyone. I reminded myself I would leave without explanation at the first sign of anything dark or dangerous. He didn't seem surprised to see me. He didn't seem like he was in a hurry. Like he was just happy to be spending time with a beautiful woman. He was playful and reassuring. Our conversation flowed with ease. We even talked about the Sadist. He responded with anger toward the harm I had suffered and offered comfort and reassurance that he cared most about my needs. It didn't take long for me to lose all resistance and allow him to gently take control. It felt good to be handled with care. To feel beautiful and desirable again.

I wasn't just choosing him because he was unavailable. I was choosing him because he made my own unavailability feel justified.

Sometime the next morning, as I lay in the most relaxed state I'd felt in years, wrapped in his arms, he catches me studying him a bit.

"Oh, you're in trouble."

"Who, me? Why do you say that... Sir?"

"I could get really used to this. But be careful. Don't fall in love with me. I can see it in your eyes." I burst into laughter.

"That's just the raging hormones, sir. I'm clear on what this is. That's why I'm here. Unfettered fantasy with a clear exit strategy."

"You're here because I want you here. Now get in the shower and wait. I'll join you shortly."

I obeyed. When we kissed goodbye that morning, I didn't know when I would see him again.

"I'll call you soon. Wait for me."

I chuckled inside, believing there was a good chance I would never speak to him again. Clearly, he had other plans. Four days later he was back on another customer visit. Then again 3 days later. What started as a single pit stop became a regular detour. Every time he was back in town, he reached out. Every time, I said yes. We never played house. We played hotel. Kept it compartmentalized. Cordial. Even caring, in its own odd way.

He was charming. Smooth. He knew how to make a woman feel wanted. He knew how and where to push me, so I maintained my agency while being able to completely surrender. Maybe that's what I was wanting after all—to be the one someone couldn't wait to see again, even if only for a night.

It wasn't cheating. It wasn't love. It was something else entirely: An adult thrill disguised as a dream worth keeping.

I wanted this. I wanted what this was doing for me and the freedom I felt when we were together. This was everything I was looking for and more.

Finally, a bungalow option that works.

Six weeks later, he turned to me in the soft post-coital quiet and said:

"I need you. I love you. I want more."

I froze. That wasn't the agreement. That wasn't the assignment. That breaks the arrangement. I brushed it off as an emotional outburst on his part. Guess he's the one who should have been more careful.

"You have a wife," I said, half-joking, half-horrified. "She might have something to say about a change in the arrangement."

But when he just looked at me, eyes full of desire and need, I knew he was serious. Playtime was over. There had never been any arrangement—and I knew it. I demanded full honesty right then and there.

He complied.

Told me he'd told her he wasn't happy. Told me his kids weren't young anymore. He'd only said that to avoid attracting women who'd expect too much of him. Told me about the affair they had survived and relocated over once before. Told me I had brought him clarity.

"You showed me what I really want," he said. "It's time to start chasing that… with you."

And, okay. I was flattered. Intrigued. Still single and enjoying the chemistry. I even enjoyed keeping him company on the phone during long work trips.

But by the time he returned for his next visit, I knew I needed to draw the line. This spring fling needed to end before real damage was done.

So, I agreed to see him one more time.
I told myself it was closure.
I didn't let him take control. I had things to say first.

"I can't do this anymore. We've been having a lot of fun, and I've grown really attached to you, but this is all fantasy. Trying to move this outside our bubble will never work. I don't believe that you've thought this all the way through. I just came here to say goodbye."

His response was unexpected.

He doubled down. Described a vision of life together that he had mapped out: Hot chocolate on Christmas morning as a family (all the kids), summers on the lake enjoying his new boat, and work conferences where we could both work remotely and enjoy more hotel nights along with romantic adventures all over the world.

He didn't just want to live life without me in it, he wanted to build something together.

If only all those things weren't what I wanted too. If only all the time spent together over the last two months hadn't been near perfect. If only I hadn't come to trust and enjoy having him in the driver's seat. If only he was single. If only I had walked out of the room and never looked back.

If this were fiction, that's exactly what I would have done.

But instead, I let myself believe him. I let myself feel loved. I justified it all. Despite the risk. Despite the cost.

I began negotiating new boundaries and expectations with him, needing more details about life at home. The weeks that followed were peppered with hopeful updates. He was promised a promotion that would take him off the road and let him work remotely with the occasional in-person trip or work conference, just like my job. Even when I said I wouldn't want him moving out of her house and directly in with me, he agreed and had a plan for how to transition everything to make me comfortable.

Now when he came to town, he would stay in a hotel but spend the afternoons at my house. He met a few of my friends. We talked every day. We began crafting the narrative that would set this relationship up for future success. Something that would defy the odds. It felt like a normal dating relationship with a simple exception—he was still married. But I had looked past that this long, surely, I could see it through. Even though it felt different now. Like we were lying. Like I was breaking up a family. Even if that's what he said he wanted.

My friends were increasingly concerned. Some flat out said they were against the whole thing and wouldn't support us until he was fully divorced or at least had papers filed. It was going exactly as he said it would go. Until it didn't.

The promotion didn't come through. You know, the one that was supposed to make everything possible? But he kept trying. Kept planning, laying groundwork. Looking for the right time to end a 20+ year relationship.

Then, he had a major health crisis and landed in the hospital followed by weeks of recovery at home. Texts and calls were relegated to social media DMs so the wife wouldn't see them. I found myself waiting. A lot.

Psycho Self started offering her assistance regularly. She had all kinds of ideas … If he couldn't or wouldn't follow through, I could just swing by his house. Join his wife's favorite hobby club online and befriend her somehow. Call his best friend and enlist supporters. Have a friend of mine confront him. Or the classic—send a letter to the wife exposing everything… Just to name a few.

Instead, I took to journaling all the things I would say to him if we were actually talking as regularly as we had been. The sweet and the sour stuff. Anything from him would have sustained my support and connection: Take the next step and hire an attorney. Tell her and file. At the very least, move into the guest bedroom! But none of it was happening.

I was unraveling and finally one trusted friend, wise and unafraid, called bullshit.

"Haven't you been the wife in this scenario?" She asked. "You're better than being the woman who's lied to, even if the lie is dressed up like honesty."

And just like that, the fog lifted.

I was standing in a full circle moment where I was now the woman who an unhappily married man had cheated with.

It wasn't the same circumstance as the infidelity that happened in my marriage, but it was infidelity all the same. I could no longer hold myself as better than my ex and the women he cheated with. Sure, sure, it was different. We didn't have an arrangement. He lied.

But really, who's to say my married man really did either. I had just accepted his lies to meet my own needs. And somewhere along the line I started lying to myself as well.

This is what I warned him about when I tried to end it months ago.

This is messy and having been through my own divorce, and supported others through theirs. It all takes time, and a lot of individual reckoning. I had been willing to help support him through it. What I couldn't do anymore was lie to myself.

And the truth was obvious: this wasn't the man I had been hoping for. This was the moment I had been avoiding. The moment where I had to choose what I was worth. I had done this to myself. I knew what it was, and I made choices along the way to bring me to this point. It was time to make different choices.

So, I set a simple deadline. He missed it. I set another one. Missed it again. Our visits became a little less frequent. Our texts and calls became a little shorter and more spread out. The topic of his marriage dominated our conversations. This wasn't fun anymore. So, the next time he called, I decided not to wait anymore.

"I've got to say something."

"I know you do. I'm sorry it's been so long since we've talked. Things here just seem impossible right now. Nothing is happening the way I thought it would. I still love you. We are going to be together."

"I love you too. I want to believe all of that, and I want to believe I can be patient. But I can't. This whole situation is turning me into a sniveling mistress hiding in the shadows desperate for our next interaction. I won't live that way and either I create distance for myself or keep waiting until neither one of us finds me attractive. Take care of your health. Take care of your family. *Call me when you're single.*"

I waited for a couple months just to see if he would. He didn't. It was time to let go. So, I took the time to write him a letter that would never get sent. I burned the journal pages I had filled waiting for him to call.

The emotional toll of this one was palatable. What had started as a simple flirtation to take my mind off darker days, was now causing me a whole new kind of pain. What I had allowed into my life as a source of comfort and pleasure, was now compromising what was left of my character. What had fueled a fantasy had only served to drain the last of my pride.

There was no one to blame but myself. I mean, sure, I have plenty to hold against him, but in some ways, I had gotten exactly what I went looking for and more. In some ways, I suppose it was "fun while it lasted," but the fun was over. I had come face to face with what I was capable of. The woman looking back at me in the mirror had finally removed her romance-colored glasses. I didn't want to do any more field research. My heart couldn't take it. I deserved better.

## INSIGHT UNCOVERED:

**You don't have to be lied to, to be deceived.**

And sometimes you are the one doing the lying–to yourself.

Sex is the easy part. Connection is harder. Commitment? That's something else entirely.

Through this charming traveler's eyes, I finally saw how infidelity doesn't always start with betrayal. It starts with loneliness.

And with that, I gained a deeper compassion for how my ex-husband might have slipped outside the bounds of our marriage. Not because it was right, but because now I knew just how easy it could be. I wasn't naive. I was hopeful. This time, hope wasn't enough to save me. It was, however, enough to teach me where my integrity actually lived.

And in that hope, I let convenience override clarity. I ignored what I knew and embraced what I wanted to believe.

But the most sobering truth? I might not have been breaking promises to a spouse, but I was breaking them to me.

I'm simply not interested in dishonest relationships anymore. Especially not with myself.

## CASE FILE No. 07

# ACROSS THE UNIVERSE

- LONG-DISTANCE DELIRIUM
- EMOTIONAL ARSON
- STAR-CROSSED SWIPING

**CASE STATUS:**

TRANSFERRED OUT OF ROMANCE

# 07:
# ACROSS THE UNIVERSE

**Alias: The Twin Flame**

---

**CHARGES:**

Long-Distance Delirium, Emotional Arson, Star-Crossed Swiping

**CASE STATUS:**

Burned Bright. Burned Out. Transcended Romance.

---

I woke up with a weight lifted. I was no longer tethered to the Married Man. I had finally given myself the gift of closure.

Naturally, I opened my go-to app and there he was. Handsome. Warm eyes. A magnetic stillness. My heart leapt. Then I hesitated. My inner critic whispered, "A guy like that isn't into girls like you."

Then came my best friend's voice, loud and true: "Don't make their decision for them. If you find them attractive, swipe right."

I laughed. After everything I'd been through in modern dating, you would think I'd outgrown that insecurity. But old voices linger.

So, I swiped right.

And wouldn't you know it? He had already "super liked" me! I tried to play it cool. Then, I started the conversation. I offered to meet for lunch the next day as I passed through his town. He declined. Not because he wasn't interested, but because he already had plans with his daughter and wasn't going to flake on her.

Green flag.

Then another Green flag: He preferred to take things slowly. He wanted connection before chemistry. Conversation before momentum. So, we scheduled a video call. He was even more attractive in real time. Genuine, attentive, and just as surprised by our chemistry as I was.

During one of our early conversations, he asked if I liked to read. I said yes. Then he asked if I'd ever want to read a book with someone, out loud or silently, to discuss and learn together. I laughed out of pure delight. But he flinched, mistaking it as mockery. Apparently, other women had laughed at the idea. I quickly reassured him he had just leveled up the kind of woman he was talking to.

Had I really tripped over an emotionally available, financially stable, spiritually grounded, dedicated father after everything I'd crawled through? It felt like fate. We allowed ourselves to enjoy the process. Stayed in the present moment. But I could feel it happening. I was falling. Fast. Again.

His words suggested he was too. I hadn't felt spiritual compatibility like this in nearly a decade.

***Enter: My Twin Flame***

They say a twin flame isn't meant to last. They're meant to ignite. To expose. To consume every part of you that isn't healed and hand it back in ashes.

From the beginning, it felt cosmic. We shared a deep spirituality. One formed by the church but no longer confined to it. We had both walked through enough fire to find wonder in other places too. Nature. Energy. Mystery. From our very first call, it felt familiar. Like meeting someone in this life who had already loved you in another.

The language of spiritual alignment became our shorthand. We pulled birth charts. Read scripture. It felt like more than flirtation. Something more than compatibility. It felt like recognition. It felt like kindling.

He even planned our first date around a solar eclipse. Packed a picnic, pre-ordered glasses, printed prayer rituals. The in-person connection was electric. Deep. Magical. Gazing into his eyes was like staring into the super charged sky. When we kissed in the park that day, we were both physically blown backward by the force of it.

But what surprised me most wasn't the spark. It was the ease. I didn't have to try. I just had to show up fully myself. He didn't try to impress or over-promise. He told the truth. About where he was, what he could offer, and what he couldn't. He wasn't looking for someone save him. He was looking for someone to *see* him. To walk beside him, not carry him.

He admired that I had raised a daughter. That I didn't need rescuing. That we could choose each other out of desire, not dependency.

His daughter was the same age mine had been at the start of my hardest co-parenting years. The parallels were uncanny. Watching him show up for her with consistency and softness stirred something deep in me. Getting to support him as a father was healing something in me.

"What do you think your life will look like in 10 years?"

Somehow his simple question stopped me in my tracks. Ten years ago, I thought I'd be married again by now. Or at least in a relationship where we were counting down the days to our empty nest adventures. What could I say with certainty now? The truth was anything but romantic.

"Well, let's see. I expect I'll have lost one, if not both, of my parents. Same with at least one of my dogs. Maybe I'll be a grandmother by then. Maybe I'll be watching my daughter walk down the aisle."

He felt my tone shift and said, "Sounds like you'll need a soft place to land and a steady shoulder. If you need one, I'm here. I'm going to need some parenting support. I've got the teen years ahead and I'm not ready."

It resonated as real life companionship and support through the joys and tragedies that were waiting for us in the years ahead.

What I cherished most were the quiet, ordinary moments: cooking together, sitting on the porch, laughing at the cat, watching butterflies in the yard. It was peaceful. Present. Unremarkable in the best way.

We even built our own rituals. He called them "Slow Burn Sundays."

Whether together or apart, we'd share coffee, breakfast, a spiritual check-in, and curl up in a cozy spot to read a book to one another.

When we talked, it felt like we didn't have to explain ourselves the same way we did with our exes. We could talk about anything. Ask each other anything. It became like a little sacred rhythm: one-part sabbath, one-part domestic fantasy. Safe and steady even when things got hard.

I remember one Sunday in the fall, he stepped in from the back patio and said quietly, "Darlin', there's something wrong with your dog. He's not doing well. You may need to prepare yourself."

I was stunned.

My sweet dog Princeton had lost weight, but I thought he had it to spare. A few short days later, I had to put him down. I was wrecked, but grateful. My Twin Flame had seen what I hadn't. He didn't try to fix it. He just stayed present. Honest. Steady.

Many evenings, we would sit by the fire wrapped in each other. When we were apart, we would still talk on the phone for hours. We enjoyed sharing the little things that gave special meaning to our days. Like watching sunsets together and noticing when a ladybug would land nearby as we talked. We shared deeper hurts we'd both carried and survived. We gave each other grace for the hurt we had caused others.

Together, we would release old attachments. Burn photos, letters and other things that helped us let go. Pray together. Hold one another. Not with answers, but with permission to feel deeply. Cry loudly. Ask boldly. He reminded me to trust myself. To stop outsourcing my wisdom. To listen to the still, small voice I'd been working so hard to believe. He came to rely on me to help calm the chaos in his own heart too.

For a while, those moments of magic fueled our alignment.

There was no obvious turning point. No siren. No weather alert. One moment we were in a flow. The next, in a flurry. What first captured our imaginations began to overwhelm our senses. It would start innocently enough. Spiritual musings, deep dives, cosmic connections. But eventually, if my answers didn't quell his questions or ease his inner chaos, things would escalate. He would shift from inquiry into interrogation. Demanding I keep trying, keep listening until he was satisfied.

I told myself it was just the whiskey. Just the occasional bad night. If it got to be too much, I'd excuse myself. Go inside. Hang up the phone.

Until the night it followed me.

We were at his house, tucked in for a winter weekend. We'd been drinking, laughing, chasing warmth and sparks by the fireplace. He stepped outside for a smoke, and I stayed behind grabbing a robe from his closet, curling up in front of the fire, letting my guard drop. When he returned, something had shifted. He didn't join me to snuggle. He sat beside me and stared. Agitated. Distant. He looked at me, then the robe.

"What are you wearing? You can't wear that. It's not right."
I was confused. I had grabbed it instinctively.
"It's cold," I offered. "Do you want it?"
He shook his head. "No. I'd rather burn it."
"What?! Why? I don't understand."
"It was hers. I don't want anything of hers getting on you."

And then he reached over me. Took it off my body. Tossed it straight into the fire.

I sat frozen. Not because of the fire. But because of the fury. I tried to soothe him. To reach him. To understand. But that night, he was unreachable. Loud. Accusatory. Spun up.

And suddenly, I wasn't in his living room anymore. I was back in my marriage. Back in the scenes I swore I'd never revisit. The rants. The confusion. The emotional volatility. The helpless feeling of being trapped in someone else's storm.

That night, I cried myself to sleep alone. He didn't remember much the next morning, just asked if he really burned the robe. He didn't recall the tears. The trembling. He apologized for being "a little intense." But I couldn't quite shake the emotional hangover.

In the quiet of my drive home, I knew. This couldn't go on forever. It felt cosmic. It felt meaningful. But it also felt like a familiar pattern I'd already survived.

And for the first time in a long time, I knew I didn't have to repeat it. I just had to choose what was best for me and decide how to respond.

Would I just ghost him and never go back? Would I break up with him because of my own past hurts? Would I decide to give it another chance and navigate these rough waters? After all, this was my twin flame. He was different. I was different.

It didn't feel like it was over. Even if we weren't going to last forever, the least we could do is let this run its course and not cut it short out of fear.

He never acted that way when he wasn't drinking. For my own sake, I wanted to show myself I could show up differently than I had in the past. So, we talked about it, made agreements about how we would hold boundaries differently going forward. Most importantly, I committed to myself, that if he ever came close to crossing that line again, I would stand my ground instead of abandoning myself.

Where I had previously frozen, with him I confronted.
Where I had previously fawned, with him I corrected.

I stopped trying to fix him. I would just call him back to himself and the agreements we had made to be painfully honest with ourselves and each other, to not punish each other for past partners' hurts, and to be curious and not accusatory.

Until I found my footing, these moments were chaotic and caustic.

Once grounded and empowered, they were cleansing. It felt like evidence of the healing I had already done and of the healing we were both experiencing together.

We were back in a flow.

Our twin flame dynamic was back in full effect. I had experienced spiritual resonance with other people, but this connection was unique. An energetic tether that allowed us to reach each other from any distance.

I'll never forget the time, after ending a late-night phone call with him, I couldn't fall asleep. Every time I closed my eyes it felt like he was there beside me, asking if I was still awake. I shook it off. I was just overthinking, overstimulated from the call. After thirty minutes of that, I finally sat up and sent him a text.

"Where are you right now?" I asked, "Are you doing something?"
"I'm on the front porch. I'm not doing anything," he replied.
"You're not doing anything? Because it feels like you're not letting me sleep, like you keep yelling at me to talk to you or something."
"Holy shit! It worked."

Excuse me?? What worked?!"

Sure enough, he'd been on his front porch, yelling into the sky for me to talk to him. He was wide awake and nowhere near done with our conversation.

And somehow—I heard him. I ***felt*** him.

I called and finished the conversation. Another storm had passed. Another portal opened.

We started to experiment a bit with the energetic connection we discovered that night. Turns out it's typical for twin flames to hear each other because they are actually a part of you. Hearing them is like hearing your own internal voice. We could anticipate each other. Operate openly from our intuition.

It was exciting. Exhilarating. At first. Then it became a bit exhausting for both of us. I'd be tired and he would want to keep going. He would be tired and I would want to keep going.

Weekend visits became beautiful, borrowed time. We'd cram intimacy into 48 hours, high on connection, low on sleep, pretending we weren't starting to fray. We'd part ways, exhausted, with a strange mix of contentment and grief.

The classic push-pull dynamic of twin flames had us in its grip.

The time together that once refueled us began to require more than we had to give. I left his house feeling emptier than when I arrived. When he left mine, the high of being together would meet its low. During his drives home, like clockwork, the pendulum would swing from intimate to detached.

The time together was getting overshadowed by the distance. Living 250 miles apart had always been a challenge. He said from day one that he didn't date outside his zip code, but something about me felt worth the exception.

But now, he was increasingly worried about missing time with his daughter. He began resenting the toll the trips were taking on his body, his car, his budget, his bandwidth. Truthfully, I was too. I just wasn't ready to let go just yet.

I was clinging to the magic.

And I did what I do when I'm afraid. I pushed through it. I was convinced if I just showed up hard enough—emotionally, logistically, spiritually—I could close the gap between us. Surely the stars would open the door for us to take the next step. Surely this wasn't meant to end in heartache after all we had fought through to get to this point. I had all but forgotten the deep clarity that he wasn't my forever.

When he declared that he wouldn't be coming back, I didn't want to listen. I didn't want to hear him say that. I was tired of hearing people I knew loved me, and whom I loved, say that it wasn't going to work. That they weren't enough or weren't ready or whatever. I wanted what I wanted, and I was convinced he wanted it too. Because he said he did. We had both invested so much.

So, I pushed back. Stood my ground. Held the mirror up believing this was just another storm to weather. Instead, it became more tumultuous. More combative and confrontational.

His next visit was his last. I was still welcome to come, but instead of the warm and peaceful comfort of his arms upon arrival, I was met with exhaustion and tolerance. The tone of our phone and text communication shifted. He was done. He was pushing me out. For good. It took weeks, but I finally surrendered.

"Please come get your things and forget about this place," he said

"I have nothing to collect," I responded, "Give my things to your daughter or throw them away."

And just like that, where there was a flame, only ashes remained. I had no fight left. No magic left to fix it.

I want to say I should have listened to him sooner. Let him go easier. Not been so attached. I already knew in my soul it wasn't built to last. But I will never regret fighting for someone I love. As long as I'm not the only one fighting. I wasn't begging for him to love me. He confirmed that time after time. He just didn't have any more to give. It was over.

And while I sat in the dark shadow of another failed love affair, I saw the cold truth of my patterns. I saw how he and I had played our parts perfectly. I saw how strong I had become, despite my weaknesses and limitations. I saw myself in his reflection.

We had been honest. Fully ourselves. True twin flames.

After our breakup, we didn't talk for months. Complete radio silence. I needed the time and space to detach. Ground myself and reflect.

But I could still feel him sometimes. Like a silent energetic thread tethered to memory. I didn't reach out when it happened. But I had a sense we were safe from the storm. I wanted to reach out but wanted to navigate it safely. Not just keep my heart on hold for a reprise. So, I turned to research for comfort.

I read about the kind of bond we had named from the beginning: twin flames. I read about the passion, the volatility, the chaos and clarity. How this kind of connection could ignite healing or burn everything down. Twin flames hold the power to facilitate healing for one another, but only if they're willing.

Healing doesn't happen by accident. It requires consent. Intention. And we had that. For a while.

Is it possible to let what was good about us transcend romance? It had worked with the Introvert and the Singer. Was I trying to convince myself when all I really wanted was to try again? Was there a pull or was I just being indulgent?

I decided to trust my intuition and reach out during the next eclipse.

Just a simple message acknowledging the cosmic connection. We were supposed to watch this eclipse together. He responded within minutes. He was thinking of me that day too. It was clear the love was still there for both of us. We talked for a while and didn't run from the pain of our shared past, but neither of us were interested in repeating any cycles. Our reasons for breaking up were still reasons.

We became friends—but only at a distance. Close enough to honor what had been, far enough to keep from pretending it could be something else. An occasional text, song, or prayer request. Even a shared cup of coffee over the phone on a slow Sunday.

As time passed, we talked less and less. The desire to revisit our romance never resurfaced.

He was there for me when my mom's health kept getting worse. I was his first call when his mom unexpectedly passed. And when my mom died, he gave me space.

Somehow, I could be my saddest, darkest, honest self around him. I knew he wouldn't try to make me feel better or explore the deeper truths. He would just sit in it with me or leave me alone to face the fire.

When I found the files from my divorce. You know, the ones that started this whole case review? He was one of the few people I called. Not because I needed him to fix anything, but because I knew he would understand what I needed to do without asking.

"Do you want to come here and burn it?"
"You read my mind. I'll check my calendar."

I arrived a few weeks later, files in hand, having reviewed them in detail with my best friend and therapist. He and I read through some of the pages. Laughed. Cried. Marveled at how far I had come since then.

In that safe space, where love resided, I let go. I let go of my past, my pattern, and took in the power of the present moment. Watching the pages burn, he sat beside me like he had done many times before.

This time as a friend. A flame keeper.

## INSIGHT UNCOVERED:

Some love stories don't end. They transform.

They leave behind no clear villain, no neat conclusion. Just a scorched trail of passion, growth, and spiritual excavation.

I used to believe that if a connection was real, it would last. That if someone saw your soul, they would stay.

But I've come to understand something softer, something deeper:

Some souls are only meant to walk with us part of the way. To mirror our fire. To stoke our awakening. To help us shed who we're not so we can remember who we are.

That doesn't make it a failure. That makes it sacred.

He saw me and I saw him. Even when we couldn't hold on, we never let go of the truth:

**We were real.**

And real love doesn't need proximity to leave a mark. It just needs honesty. And sometimes, distance.

Because not every spiritual bond requires a shared life.
Sometimes the healing continues after letting go.
Real love lasts through the magic and the melancholy.

# CLOSING ARGUMENTS

# CLOSING ARGUMENTS

## The Truth I Found

---

I didn't know when I would reach the last case file. But once the Twin Flame burned out and silence settled in, something shifted. I didn't need to collect more stories. The urgency to find "the one" went quiet. Not out of cynicism but because, for the first time in years, I wasn't looking for someone else to carry my story forward. I was ready to look back, connect the dots, and finally ask the only question that mattered:

What was I trying to prove by staying in the pattern so long?

The last file's been closed. The lovers have left the building. Now it's just me, a stack of confessions, and the truth I am finally ready to face.

If the pattern keeps repeating, I'm not just the victim.
I'm the accomplice.

Investigations rarely begin with certainty. You follow the evidence, hoping it tells you something true. By the time things ended with my Twin Flame, I hadn't given up on love, just the grind of collecting red flags like souvenirs. I was worn out.

No need to chase another mystery just to gather more evidence.

Finding that old case file from my divorce wasn't an accident. It was Exhibit A.

My pattern had always been there. I just hadn't been ready to see it. But when I finally did, it brought enough light to offer forgiveness to my ex…and compassion to myself. The line from the file still echoes:

***"You're amazing. You've always deserved better."***

I believed the first part. I finally had enough evidence to believe the second. Just because I don't need much doesn't mean I deserve the bare minimum. Their words weren't lies, but their actions told the truth.

That gap between desire and capacity? That's not about my worth. It's about their limits—and respecting mine.

I stopped trying to convince others to rise to the moment. I chose to be better for myself.

The final step in this cold case analysis? Calling court back into session for an honest reckoning of every red flag and romantic fatality I could no longer explain away. One last walk through the evidence. The suspects. The witnesses. And, finally, a cross examination of myself before the verdict is read.

# THE SUSPECTS

Let the record show: Each man, each relationship, served a purpose in the long-running investigation of my heart. Some lightning strikes. Others slow burns. A few that never caught fire.

But each name in the file—The IT Guy, The Painter, The Diabetic, The Introvert, The Married Man, The Twin Flame, The Singer—holds a vital clue in identifying the pattern.

Not just in who they were toward me, but in how I showed up in the relationship dynamic. I'm convinced they would testify to certain facts differently. Some may not remember me at all. But each of them left fingerprints on my heart.

The IT Guy proved that I keep promises to those I love, no matter where life takes us. The Diabetic reminded me that sweet beginnings can still leave a bitter aftertaste. The Painter awakened my weakness for fantasy over function, but it will never build a life. The Married Man was my turning point. A full circle moment where I realized I kept accepting crumbs in place of commitment.

The Twin Flame burned through every illusion, every lie I told myself about what love should look like. The Singer helped me find my voice and my faith again. Healing happened in perfect harmony. Not a lover, but a lifeline. The Introvert showed me the courage to keep promises to myself first, even if it means choosing partnership over passion.

Not all of them hurt me. Not all of them healed me.
All of them helped me map the terrain between self-abandonment and self-acceptance.

A word about the Diplomat and the Sadist. Both left evidence I'd rather exclude from the trial. Their files are darker, impact heavier. They don't belong in the same case file drawer as the others.

They proved that dating is risky. Trusting strangers can be dangerous. Staying open to love while guarding your heart and body from harm is like walking a tightrope. I don't want to close myself off from new relationships, but I never want to play a polite princess in the face of predatory behavior. Behavior like that doesn't deserve patience, understanding, nor diplomacy.

I was fortunate that these examples didn't rise to the level of criminality or leave more permanent scars on my body, as many encounters for women in modern dating do. What I learned from these men are lessons I never want to repeat.

They, and the Crime Spree, also expose a level of recklessness in my actions I cannot afford to revisit.

I don't regret any of it. I don't shame the version of me who searched. She needed to. She was doing fieldwork. Testing theories. Gathering evidence. Building a case for her own damn dignity. And in the end, she got it.

I have no interest in prosecuting the men in these files. I'm not here to indict them. My opinions of their actions are my own. Their investigations are their own. I'm here to expose the patterns that kept me circling the same endings.

# CHARACTER WITNESSES

Even in the grittiest investigations, there are people who help you hold the flashlight. People who show up not to rescue you, but to remind you who you are when the evidence gets muddled and the suspects start sounding like saints. In my case, those people weren't love interests. They were anchors. Mirrors. Compasses when I needed help navigating.

***Exhibit A: My Brother. The First Witness.***

My first witness in life. Whether I knew it or not, he was always watching out for me. Protecting me. The original straight shooter, especially from a man's perspective. He never claimed to understand everything I was going through, but he didn't need to. He loved me. He never dissected my dating life, but he never let me forget who the hell I was when someone else tried to make me smaller. He was always willing to go into battle with and for me. A quiet force, but never silent when it mattered.

***Exhibit B: My Gay Soulmate. The Mirror.***

The stage manager turned soul-friend. The one who sang harmony before I could find my melody again. He never tried to fix me. Just sat beside me in the silence until I felt safe enough to sing. When I questioned whether I was lovable, he never argued. He just looked at me like it was obvious. His presence reminded me that spiritual connection doesn't have to come dressed in romance to be sacred.

***Exhibit C: My Daughter. The Anchor.***

The firecracker. The fierce one. The girl with more backbone at sixteen than I had at thirty-five. She didn't sit quietly in the wings. She sat front row, popcorn in one hand, a raised eyebrow in the other, fully invested and never afraid to say, "Mom, absolutely not." She had strong opinions and no patience for men who brought weak effort. She was affected. She was vocal. And she reminded me daily what was at stake. She didn't let me settle. Not for long, anyway.

***Exhibit D: My Best Friends. The Vault.***

The vaults. The women who always answer the phone, no matter the hour, no matter the story. They've heard every messy detail, every excuse I made for men who didn't deserve them, and never once made me feel small for caring too much. Okay, maybe just enough to snap me out of it. Only when I needed it. They made sure I was clear about who the asshole was—even if, on occasion, it was me. They reminded me not to give up on love, or myself. To get back up when heartbreak knocked the wind out of me. And I did the same for them. Divorces, breakups, self-sabotage, career navigation, and child-rearing. We've coached each other through it all. Always with laughter, tears, and a favorite beverage on tap.

***Exhibit E: My Mentor. The Guide.***

She didn't just hand me a pen at her retreat. She handed me back my voice. She saw something in me I was only beginning to see in myself. She helped me craft a personal mission statement: "To identify, communicate, and integrate ***truth*** for myself and others." That line was more than ink. It was a declaration. A north star. Over the years, as we discussed everything from family to franchises, she would remind me never to lose my center. Eventually, I came to realize I didn't need to be fully healed to be honest.

***Exhibit F: Me. The Final Witness.***

Yes, me. The version of me who did what it took to get out of a damaging marriage. The one who waged a war on shame and learned to love someone who previously felt unworthy of it. The one who got back in the car after bad dates. Who cried, journaled, and still showed up to the next encounter with hope. The one who learned not just what she wanted, but what she'd never tolerate again. Even when she held on a little too long, worked a little too hard, or gave a little too much… She was never weak. Just gathering testimony. It's time she takes the stand.

These are the people—the moments, the mirrors—that reflected what I was too fogged up to see on my own. Their love was the evidence I needed to believe in something better. It was worth dusting myself off, straightening my spine, and getting back to the case. Not to chase someone else, but to build a future rooted in truth. Something real. Something aligned. Something mine.

# SELF-CROSS EXAMINATION

Let's be clear. I wasn't always the wronged party in every scene. I played prosecutor, sure, but sometimes, I was also the unreliable witness. The one who withheld evidence, ignored red flags, twisted the facts to fit a more comfortable story. Sometimes, I was the one holding the smoking gun of my own unmet expectations.

So now I turn the spotlight fully on myself, and I ask:

- Why did you stay when you already knew?
- What were you hoping to fix? Him or you?
- When you lowered the bar, did you call it grace to feel noble? Or survival to feel safe?
- How many times did you confuse being desired with being respected?
- When he said, "You deserve better," did you believe it or did you try to convince him to stay anyway?
- What parts of yourself did you shrink to fit someone else's version of "enough"?
- Did you mistake the drama for depth?
- Did you keep chasing closure from men who didn't even deserve a conversation?
- Were you lonely… or just avoiding being alone with yourself?

These aren't accusations. They're invitations. To remember. To be honest. To take inventory without shame.

There were times I stayed too long. Times I stayed quiet when I should have spoken. Times I flirted with fantasy, edited out the inconvenient truths, and handed over trust like it came with a refund policy. I wasn't chasing love—I was chasing validation with a flashlight and a badge. And when I didn't get it, I sometimes tried to earn it. Or worse, prove I was worth it by sticking around through the dysfunction.

I've ghosted. I've deflected. I've rationalized behavior that wasn't rational, just because I wanted the ending I'd written in my head. I've turned men into metaphors, into experiments, into measuring sticks for how much I'd healed. And when they didn't pass the test, I didn't always own that maybe the rubric was rigged.

I've mistaken chaos for chemistry. I've confused attention for affection. I've overplayed my cool when I was crumbling inside. I've made men my mission instead of staying loyal to my own.

And maybe worst of all—I've sometimes known from the first kiss, the first text, the first silence—that it wouldn't work. But I stayed anyway. Because I was hopeful. Because I was scared. Because I was lonely. Because part of me still thought I had something to prove. Because leaving early meant admitting I had chosen wrong again. And that felt heavier than staying.

So no, this isn't a clean tale of villain and victim. It's murky. Human. Flawed. That's what makes it real. That's what makes the testimony credible.

Now that the mirror's on the stand, I can see it clearly: I wasn't just surviving heartbreak, I was complicit in it. I kept putting my hope in places I had already marked "closed." I romanticized red flags and mistook compromise for character. I handed out chances as if the suspects would eventually transform themselves into a fairytale prince. I wasn't just a casualty of love gone wrong. I was the one refusing to leave the crime scene. And healing didn't start until I stopped tampering with the evidence.

It was time to stop hiding. Time to stop letting shame keep me stuck in the shadows. Because somewhere along the line, I confused shame with accountability. Let it take up residence in my gut like it had paid rent. There's a version of shame that's protective—a sharp internal pang that says, "You know better." That version invites growth. But there's another version. The parasitic kind. The shame that loops on repeat: You should have known. You should have left. You should have been better, smarter, smaller, less.

That shame doesn't build—it buries. And buried shame doesn't heal. It reenacts. It looks for new stages to replay old scripts.

I wore it like a trench coat in summer, heavy and unnecessary. I let it color how I saw myself in every mirror and every memory. I let it silence me. Shape me. Shrink me. But shame, when it's misplaced, is just fear in a nicer outfit.

So, here's the self-cross examination declaration:

I'm not here to be ruled by regret. I've done my inventory. I know what was mine to own, and what was never mine to carry in the first place.

And the rest? I'm laying it down.
Not in denial. But in dignity.

# THE VERDICT

The jury has returned from deliberation, and I've heard the testimony loud and clear. This isn't about guilt or innocence. It's about one woman's truth. And the truth is: I am no longer on trial.

I am not too much. I am not too late. I am not defined by who didn't stay or who couldn't choose me. I wasn't broken. I was rehearsing. Rehearsing abandonment. Rehearsing desirability. Rehearsing control. I kept choosing situations that mirrored unresolved questions about my worth, hoping this time I would get a different answer.

I am the one who stayed. The one who kept showing up. Who asked the hard questions. Who stopped looking for verdicts in other people's eyes and started listening to the quiet, steady truth in her own chest.

The case is closed. The evidence has been reviewed.

***The verdict is:***

I am capable of deep love and deeper healing. I am resilient. I am worthy. I am whole. Not because someone said so, but because I've done the work to know it. I am no longer accepting sentences handed down by fear, fantasy, or someone else's inability to rise. I don't need to prove my worth through another man, another spark, another heartbreak.

I have love in my life. Deep, abiding love. The kind that shows up in best friends and belted duets, text threads and car rides, long hugs and late-night truths. I remain open to the possibility that someone new might still walk in and make this part of my life click into place, but I no longer define love or success by marital status or dramatic situationships.

I've learned to stop measuring my wholeness by proximity to romance. I am not half of anything. I'm not missing a piece.

If love finds me again, it will find me living a full life.

As of writing this, I'm still single. Still unpartnered. Still unsure whether the ever-elusive partner-in-crime, last first kiss, romantic soulmate will ever arrive.

And yet—I am enough. I am not empty.

I'm no longer casting men into narrowly defined roles that serve me, nor will I twist myself into a shallow understanding of what women bring to a relationship. I believe men and women are different, yes, but both are living the human experience. Both carry common emotions, common hurts, and a shared desire to be seen, accepted, and loved.

It's time we stop punishing new people for the crimes of lovers past. It's time we slow the pace. Let human connection—not trauma, not fantasy, not fear—take center stage. Whether we're building something together or ending things after an awkward first date, let that be the baseline: Integrity. Curiosity. Kindness.

That's what I'm taking with me, and that's what I'll keep choosing. Even if I'm the only one in the room who does.

I've served my time. I've earned my freedom.

This court is adjourned.

# CASE CLOSED

UNMET EXPECTATIONS
FANTASY vs. FUNCTION
EMOTIONAL AVAILABILITY
TRUTH

# READER'S NOTE

---

If you made it here, Thank You.
For reading, for listening, for staying with me through the crime scenes and the courtroom, the make-outs and the meltdowns.
Maybe you saw yourself in these pages. Maybe not.
But if you've ever been caught between wanting to be chosen and learning to choose yourself, you're not alone. If you've ever gotten up from heartbreak without a road map, just instinct and grit, you've already survived more than most.

This wasn't a story about men. Or even dating. It was about truth. About the work it takes to show up for yourself, so you have something real to offer someone else. To know when you're ready, and when you're not. And to recognize that being alone is not the same as being unloved.

Whatever your story looks like, I hope you walk away from this book with a little less shame, a little more clarity, and one unshakable truth: you don't have to audition for love you already deserve.
You are not behind. You are not broken. You are not too late.
Now go write your next chapter.

# ABOUT THE AUTHOR

A.K. Warren is a writer, speaker, and recovering romantic with a bachelor's degree in marketing, a master's degree in organizational development, and a doctorate in hard-earned wisdom. Her work blends storytelling, self-reflection, and sharp-eyed humor to explore what happens when love, hope, and human patterns collide.

She lives in Texas, where she spends her days building brands, mentoring women, and occasionally deleting dating apps just to re-download them an hour later. Her writing has been called "uncomfortably honest," "devastatingly funny," and "exactly what I needed to hear."

This is her first book. It probably won't be her last.

**Contact Info: akwarrenauthor@gmail.com | IG: @a.k.warren**

# NEXT IN THE SERIES

## True Crime of Modern Dating: Girlfriend Edition

These aren't my stories. They're the case files passed across brunch tables and group texts. The ones with alibis, bad decisions, and clean getaways. Because sometimes the warning signs are clearer when it's not your heart on the line. This installment is a tribute to the emotional detectives we all become when our best friend starts falling for someone new—or falling apart.

# JOIN THE INVESTIGATION

## Be your own emotional detective.

---

These questions are for book clubs, brave solo readers, or anyone willing to hold up a magnifying glass to their own patterns with grace and curiosity. There are no right answers. Just honest ones.

1. What pattern or truth in Amanda's story felt most familiar to you? Was it a certain relationship dynamic? A moment of clarity? A struggle?
2. In "Self-Cross Examination," Amanda names the ways she both caused and experienced harm. How do you relate to the idea of being both the villain and the victim in your own story?
3. One of the central themes is the difference between desire and capacity. How have you seen that play out in your own relationships? Have you ever wanted to be enough for someone who wasn't emotionally available?
4. The chapter title is "Closing Arguments: The Truth I Found." What truth(s) have you found in your own journey that you once resisted?
5. Shame shows up in Amanda's journey in subtle and loud ways. What kind of shame have you carried that wasn't yours to hold? What has helped you release it?
6. Amanda redefines success outside of marriage or dramatic romance. How do you define love and relationship success for yourself today?
7. What role have friendships played in your growth? Who are your character witnesses?
8. If you wrote your own "verdict" at this point in life, what would it say?
9. What parts of this story made you laugh, cringe, or nod in agreement? And what parts challenged you?
10. If you could tell your past-self one thing after reading this book, what would it be?

**Bonus prompt:** If you're reading this with a group, have each person write their own one-sentence "final confession" and share it with a partner in crime.

www.ingramcontent.com/pod-product-compliance
Lightning Source LLC
LaVergne TN
LVHW010656110826
845149LV00014B/3124

*9798994342206*